ISBN 978-1-390-31472-4
PIBN 11149639

1 MONTH OF
FREE
READING

at

www.ForgottenBooks.com

By purchasing this book you are eligible for one month membership to ForgottenBooks.com, giving you unlimited access to our entire collection of over 1,000,000 titles via our web site and mobile apps.

To claim your free month visit:

www.forgottenbooks.com/free1149639

English
Français
Deutsche
Italiano
Español
Português

www.forgottenbooks.com

Mythology Photography **Fiction**
Fishing Christianity **Art** Cooking
Essays Buddhism Freemasonry
Medicine **Biology** Music **Ancient
Egypt** Evolution Carpentry Physics
Dance Geology **Mathematics** Fitness
Shakespeare **Folklore** Yoga Marketing
Confidence Immortality Biographies
Poetry **Psychology** Witchcraft
Electronics Chemistry History **Law**
Accounting **Philosophy** Anthropology
Alchemy Drama Quantum Mechanics
Atheism Sexual Health **Ancient History**
Entrepreneurship Languages Sport
Paleontology Needlework Islam
Metaphysics Investment Archaeology
Parenting Statistics Criminology
Motivational

ACKNOWLEDGMENTS

I would like to thank each of my committee members, Dr.
Sheila Eyberg, Dr. Jane Pendergast, Dr. Russell Bauer, Dr.
Stephen Boggs, and Dr. Suzanne Johnson, for providing
conceptual guidance in the formulation and realization of
this project. I especially would like to thank the chair of
my committee, Dr. Eyberg, for her meticulous professional
guidance, her unfailing enthusiasm, her patience, and her
friendship during this research as throughout my graduate
training. Special thanks go to Dr. Pendergast for
her valuable statistical and editorial guidance and for
giving so freely of her time. I would also like to thank
Dr. James Algina for statistical consultation which greatly
facilitated the completion of this project.

I am grateful to Katharine Newcomb, Cheryl McNeil, and
Toni Eisenstadt for their primary contributions to this
work, and to Janet Bessmer, Gloria Medige, Laura Mee, Beth
Onufrak, Marc Wruble, and Peter Demaras for the long hours
they spent coding classroom data. I would also like to
thank the teachers who provided ratings and allowed us to
enter their classrooms.

Finally, I would like to thank family and friends who have sustained me throughout this research. My husband, Chuck, provided untold emotional support and practical assistance. My friend, Louise Kerslake, gave me peace of mind by taking such excellent care of my son while I completed this manuscript. I thank my mother, Ann White, for instilling in me a love of learning. I thank my father, James White, for teaching me not to settle for the ordinary.

TABLE OF CONTENTS

page

ACKNOWLEDGMENTS   ii

ABSTRACT.   vi

CHAPTERS

    1   INTRODUCTION   1

         Correlates of Disruptive Behavior Disorders. .   3
         Treatment of Disruptive Behavior Disorders. .   4
         School Generalization   12
         Treatment Maintenance Research Methodology. .   23
         Statement of Purpose   25
         Hypotheses   26

    2   METHOD   28

         Subjects   28
         Measures   36
         Procedures   48

    3   RESULTS   56

         Treatment Subject Analysis of Variance . . .   56
         Treatment vs. Comparison Children   81
         Comparison of Two vs. Three days
           of Classroom Observation   97

    4   DISCUSSION   101

APPENDICES

    A   PASSIVE CONSENT FORM 123

    B   COMPARISON SUBJECT SELECTION FORM 126

    C   EYBERG CHILD BEHAVIOR INVENTORY 127

    D   REVISED CONNERS TEACHER RATING SCALE 130

    E   SUTTER-EYBERG STUDENT BEHAVIOR INVENTORY. . . 132

F WALKER-McCONNELL SCALE OF SOCIAL
   COMPETENCE AND SCHOOL ADJUSTMENT:
   A SOCIAL SKILLS RATINGS SCALE FOR
   TEACHERS 135

G BODIFORD-McNEIL CLASSROOM CODING SYSTEM . . . 140

H REVISED CLASSROOM CODING SYSTEM 146

I RESEARCH PARTICIPANT CONTACT FORM 152

J INFORMED CONSENT TO PARTICIPATE IN RESEARCH. . 154

K INFORMATION RELEASE FORM FOR PERMISSION
   TO CONTACT SCHOOL 157

L ADDITIONAL INFORMATION FORM 158

M PLOTS OF SCORES BY SUBJECT ACROSS TIME 159

REFERENCES 172

BIOGRAPHICAL SKETCH 183

Abstract of Dissertation Presented to the Graduate
School of the University of Florida in Partial
Fulfillment of the Requirements for the
Degree of Doctor of Philosophy

PARENT-CHILD INTERACTION THERAPY WITH
BEHAVIOR PROBLEM CHILDREN: MAINTENANCE
OF TREATMENT EFFECTS IN THE SCHOOL SETTING

By

Beverly White Funderburk

August 1993

Chairman: Sheila Eyberg, Ph.D
Major department: Clinical and Health Psychology

Followup school assessments were conducted 12 months
and 18 months following completion of Parent-Child
Interaction Therapy, a behavioral family therapy for
preschool children with disruptive behavior disorders that
integrates traditional and behavioral methods. The 12
subjects all displayed significant home and school behavior
problems prior to treatment, and all showed clinically
significant improvement in home behavior after completing
the 14-session treatment. Ten subjects had been evaluated

in a previous school generalization study which found
significant improvements on observations and teacher ratings
of classroom conduct problem behaviors, but not on measures
of attention and activity level. In contrast to previous
reports of parent-child therapy, school generalization was
demonstrated without direct classroom intervention.

At the 12-month followup subjects maintained posttreatment improvements on observational and teacher rating
measures of classroom conduct problems and showed further
improvements in social competency. Subjects fell within the
mid-range of classroom behavior problems relative to
classroom comparison subjects on measures of conduct
problems and social competency. At the 18-month followup,
subjects maintained improvements in compliance, but
demonstrated declines on most measures into the range of
pre-treatment levels. Subjects fell at the high end of the
normal range of classroom conduct problems relative to
classroom comparison subjects at the 18-month followup.
Treatment subjects received a high rate of special
educational services at both followup assessments.

CHAPTER 1
INTRODUCTION

The Disruptive Behavior Disorders listed by DSM-III-R
include Attention-deficit Hyperactivity Disorder,
Oppositional Defiant Disorder, and Conduct Disorder
(American Psychiatric Association, 1987). Attention-deficit
Hyperactivity Disorder (ADHD), defined as having onset
before the age of seven, is characterized by a pattern of
developmentally inappropriate inattention, impulsiveness,
and hyperactivity. Oppositional Defiant Disorder (ODD) is
characterized by a pattern of developmentally inappropriate
negativistic, hostile, and defiant behavior that is usually
most evident with familiar adults. Conduct Disorder
involves a pattern of more serious violations of societal
norms, including physical aggression, truancy, theft, and
vandalism. These categories of disruptive behavior, often
grouped under the term "externalizing behaviors," are an
area of major clinical concern due to their prevalence and
prognosis.

Externalizing behavior problems account for between
one-third and three-quarters of all child referrals to
mental health agencies (Wells & Forehand, 1985). Estimates
of hyperactivity range from 3% to 15% in nonclinical samples

and to 50% and above in clinic referred youngsters (Whalen & Henker, 1991), with boys showing a higher incidence than girls. There is considerable overlap among the categories of disruptive behavior, with many children carrying more than one diagnosis (American Psychiatric Association, 1987). Longterm stability of antisocial behavior is predicted by the co-occurrence of disorders; other prognostic indicators include the density of the problem behavior, the occurrence of problem behaviors in multiple settings, and earlier age of onset (Loeber, 1982).

Despite the fact that normal preschoolers often engage in specific disruptive behaviors (Crowther, Bond, & Rolf, 1981), the pervasive patterns of behavior associated with ODD and ADHD are increasingly recognized as prognostic of later problems, even when diagnosed in the preschool age range. Campbell notes that "As a group, young hyperactive children can be differentiated from controls on measures of both core features [of ADHD] and symptoms of conduct disorder" (Campbell, 1985, p. 414). In a prospective study of children who exhibited externalizing behavior problems that persisted from age three to age six, by age nine 67% met diagnostic criteria for an externalizing disorder. At age nine, this persistent problem group also received a higher rate of special education services and mental health services than comparison groups (Campbell & Ewing, 1990).

Consistent with these findings, studies following
hyperactive boys into adolescence and early adulthood have
consistently found impaired academic achievement, continuing
attention problems, and higher rates of antisocial behavior
(Barkley, Fischer, Edelbrock, & Smallish, 1991; Fischer,
Barkley, Edelbrock, & Smallish, 1990; Mannuzza, Gittelman
Klein, & Addalli, 1991; Mannuzza, Klein, Bonagura, Malloy,
Giampino, & Addalli, 1991). It is estimated that
approximately 70% of children diagnosed with ADHD continue
to have difficulties as adolescents, regardless of whether
or not they undergo treatment with stimulant medication
(Hechtman, 1989). Overall, childhood antisocial behavior is
considered the strongest predictor of adult antisocial
behavior (Robins, 1978).

Correlates of Disruptive Behavior Disorders

Several factors have been linked with the development
of disruptive behavior disorders in children. These include
an association between lower socioeconomic status (SES) and
higher rates of problem behavior (Richman et al., 1982;
Weiss & Hechtman, 1986), and transmission of familial
patterns of antisocial behavior across generations (Robins,
1981). Negative parent-child interactions in childhood,
specifically maternal directiveness and parent-child
conflict during clinic observations, have been shown to
predict higher rates of ODD and aggression in adolescence

(Barkley et al., 1991). Maternal negative control has emerged as an important predictor variable for later behavior problems in Campbell's prospective studies of externalizing preschoolers (Campbell & Ewing, 1990; Campbell, March, Pierce, Ewing, & Szumowski, 1991). Higher rates of negative maternal control were noted even when possible maternal selection bias was controlled by selecting subjects based on teacher ratings rather than maternal report (Campbell et al., 1991).

Treatment of Disruptive Behavior Disorders

Meta-analyses of treatment outcome studies with children offer some encouragement regarding the utility of therapy for childhood psychological disorders. A meta-analysis of 105 controlled therapy outcome studies found an average effect size .79, indicating that the average treated child functioned better at posttreatment than 79% of control subjects (Weisz, Weiss, Alicke, & Klotz, 1987). A recent meta-analysis of 223 studies concurred with these findings, with a mean effect size of .88 for the subset of 64 studies that compared treatment with a no-treatment control group (Kazdin, Bass, Ayers, & Rodgers, 1990). Approximately half of the studies included in the meta-analyses addressed children with externalizing behavior disorders.

Parent Management Training

There is a wide and steadily increasing body of literature indicating that parent management training (PMT) offers great promise among therapies for externalizing disorders in pre-adolescents (Kazdin, 1987; McMahon & Wells, 1989). Broadly stated, PMT involves teaching parents new ways to interact with their children. The goal is to replace coercive patterns of interchange, which are believed to foster and sustain aggressive, oppositional child behavior, with more positive, prosocial interactions (Patterson, 1982). The therapist works primarily with parents, instructing them in social learning principles, helping them to identify and observe problem behaviors, and then to design and implement behavioral interventions in the home. A variation of PMT that is increasingly used with preschool to early elementary aged children will be referred to here as parent-child treatment. This treatment, like all variants of PMT, is based on social learning principles, but treatment incorporates direct coaching by the therapist of the parent interacting with the child in the clinic. The existing literature on PMT outcome has seldom distinguished parent-child treatment from PMT approaches that do not include the child or that target older children (Eyberg, 1992).

The effectiveness of PMT, broadly defined, for disruptive behavior disorders in children is well-documented (Kazdin, 1987; McMahon & Wells, 1989). Controlled studies have favored it over no-treatment control groups and nonbehavioral treatments (Hughes & Wilson, 1989; Pisterman et al., 1989; Taylor & Hoedt, 1974; Wells & Egan, 1988). Many studies have documented increases in child compliance, reduction of antisocial behaviors, and increases in targeted parent skills following PMT both in the clinic (e.g., Eisenstadt et al., in press; Eyberg & Robinson, 1982) and in the home (Baum & Forehand, 1981; Peed, Roberts, & Forehand, 1977). Behavioral improvements have been noted in untreated siblings as a result of treatment (Eyberg & Robinson, 1982; Humphreys, Forehand, McMahon, & Roberts, 1978). In recent years, PMT has been applied with some success in group format (Webster-Stratton & Hammond, 1990), through self-instructional bibliotherapy (Sloane, Endo, Hawkes, & Jenson, 1991), and even in therapist-absent self-administered videotape therapy (Webster-Stratton, Kolpacoff, & Hollinsworth, 1988). Studies of maintenance of treatment effects in the home have generally shown behavior at followup to be stable or slightly improved relative to the end of treatment (Forehand, Wells, & Griest, 1980; Webster-Stratton, Hollinsworth, & Kolpacoff, 1988).

Factors Affecting PMT Outcome

Much recent research effort has focused on determining factors which enhance or limit the effectiveness of PMT. Like other forms of psychotherapy, relatively high rates of drop-out and treatment failure are reported, generally in the range of 30-50% of those initiating treatment (Webster-Stratton & Hammond, 1990).

Child factors. There is some evidence that children who enter treatment at an earlier age may show better outcome and a lower treatment dropout rate than older children (Strain, Steele, Ellis, & Timm, 1982). While some evidence of maintenance of treatment effects has been shown from four to ten years following PMT treatment (Forehand & Long, 1988), it remains to be shown whether the longterm incidence of disruptive behavior disorders is lower in children who have received treatment than in those who do not receive treatment. Suggestive evidence is provided by Campbell's prospective study of disruptive children identified between the ages of two and three (Campbell & Ewing, 1990). Children whose behavior problems resolved by age six showed a lower incidence of disruptive behavior disorders (29%) at age nine than children whose problems persisted from age three through age six (67%).

An emerging issue in treatment outcome research is whether PMT may be differentially effective for ODD and

ADHD. Following treatment with Parent-Child Interaction Therapy, stronger effects were shown on observational measures of compliance than on clinic observational measures of activity and attention (Eisenstadt, Eyberg, McNeil, Newcomb, & Funderburk, in press) and in the classroom (McNeil, Eyberg, Eisenstadt, Newcomb, & Funderburk, 1991). Similar results were shown for parent training augmented with "attention training," in which parents of preschoolers were trained to increase their children's attention span by using re-focusing cues and reinforcement of on-task behavior (Pisterman et al., 1992). The results showed improved child compliance and parental acquisition of the attention training target skills, but no significant improvement in children's attention. The authors suggest "treatment of ADHD may need to take a developmental perspective. Behavioral parent training that targets compliance may be the treatment of choice during the preschool years when behavioral problems peak . . . [and] attentional problems may be more appropriately addressed during the school years if attentional problems begin to have a deleterious effect on children's academic success and classroom functioning" (Pisterman et al., 1992, p. 407).

Parent factors. Kazdin (1987) notes that PMT requires significant parent involvement and places relatively high demands on parents. Not surprisingly, factors that would be expected to limit mothers' efforts in therapy have been identified as negative predictors for therapy completion and outcome. These factors include maternal depression, increased negative life events, marital discord, and lack of social support (Compas, Howell, Phares, Williams, & Giunta, 1989; Dadds & McHugh, 1992; Webster-Stratton & Hammond, 1990). Single mothers have also been identified as at risk for poor treatment outcome (Webster-Stratton, 1992; Webster-Stratton & Hammond 1990). "Insular mothers," those who are both socially isolated and socioeconomically disadvantaged, have been identified as at exceptional risk for poor treatment outcome and maintenance (Dumas & Wahler, 1983; Wahler, 1980). Strayhorn and Weidman (1989) summarized negative predictors for PMT as follows: maternal depression, low SES, low social support, and single parent status/low father involvement. They note the dilemma that "the same characteristics predicting poor response to parent training interventions predict high risk for psychopathology in children" (Strayhorn & Weidman, 1989, p. 888).

Several modifications of PMT have attempted to ameliorate the effects of negative predictors. In a PMT program that attempted to manipulate social support, Dadds and McHugh (1992) confirmed the importance of social support as a predictor variable but were unable to increase low SES mothers' perceived social support. Another study examined different teaching methods with low SES mothers and found that the use of modeling and role playing yielded better acquisition of targeted parenting skills than verbally mediated training (i.e., reading and discussion) (Knapp & Deluty, 1989). Single mothers who received problem solving training dealing with issues other than child-rearing in addition to parent training showed more positive ratings of child's behavior four months posttreatment (Pfiffner, Jouriles, Brown, Etscheidt, & Kelly, 1990).

Parent-Child Interaction Therapy

Several characteristics of Parent-Child Interaction Therapy (PCIT) suggest its potential for achieving broad and lasting improvements in children with disruptive behavior disorders. First, it very directly targets the negative controlling maternal interactions that have been clearly linked to the development of childhood externalizing behavior problems. Second, it provides direct coaching of the parent and child interaction, which should provide for greater skills attainment in low-SES or lower functioning parents as opposed to more verbally mediated forms of parent training (Knapp & Deluty, 1989). Finally, PCIT targets the preschool age range that appears most amenable to treatment. Indeed, several studies cited above attest to the effectiveness of PCIT for treatment of externalizing behavior problems in the clinic and home environment (i.e., Eisenstadt et al., in press; Eyberg & Robinson, 1982).

Additionally, PCIT has shown promising results in the area of generalization of treatment effects into the preschool and school setting (McNeil et al., 1991), which is the primary focus of the present study. The PMT literature provides mixed findings on the issue of school generalization, and before embarking on a review of PMT school generalization studies, a brief description of Parent-Child Interaction Therapy is in order.

Parent-Child Interaction Therapy (PCIT) is a behavioral family therapy approach that integrates traditional and behavioral methods (Eyberg, 1988). Treatment is conducted in two phases, Child-Directed Interaction (CDI) and Parent-Directed Interaction (PDI). Therapy is conducted in the context of play situations, where the parent interacts with the child while a therapist coaches from behind a one-way mirror using a "bug in ear" microphone device. The primary goal of CDI is to enhance the parent-child relationship, and the parent is taught to inhibit directive and critical responses. Parents are trained to praise appropriate behavior, to follow the child's lead with behavioral imitations, verbal descriptions and reflective statements, and to ignore inappropriate behavior. In PDI, emphasis shifts to establishing effective discipline and reducing the child's noncompliance. The parent is trained to direct the child's behavior using clear, developmentally appropriate commands and to use a time-out procedure in instances of noncompliance. Generalization to the home is gradually established as the parents learn to enforce "house rules" and rules for public behavior. For a more complete description of PCIT, the interested reader is referred to Eyberg and Boggs, 1989a.

School Generalization

Studies of the generalization of behavioral improvements from the clinic setting to the school setting have been less than conclusive in the PMT literature. Most research in this area is marked by methodological flaws such as inadequate controls, unidimensional outcome assessment, and inadequate demonstration of treatment effects.

One of the earliest studies evaluating school generalization suggested the presence of a "contrast effect" of worsening school behavior simultaneous with home behavioral improvements following PMT (Johnson, Bolstad, & Lobitz, 1976). This study, however, demonstrated significant behavioral improvements in the home only on parent rating scale measures. Behavioral observation data did not indicate significant reductions in deviant behavior at home from pre- to post-treatment. Teacher rating scale assessments of eight of the children who underwent treatment showed no change from pre- to posttreatment. School behavioral observations, available on only five of the eight treatment children, revealed a nonsignificant increase in observed deviant behavior relative to a control sample of children with school behavior problems, which showed a nonsignificant decrease in observed deviant behavior. In separate small samples of children who were treated in a special educational setting, Johnson et al. (1976) observed nonsignificant increases in home deviant behavior. Combining results from the home treatment and the school treatment samples, the authors interpreted this as evidence for a behavioral contrast effect (Johnson, Bolstad, & Lobitz, 1976).

Forehand and colleagues (1979) investigated school generalization in a sample of eight children who successfully completed parent-child treatment (Forehand et al., 1979). This study reported no significant change in observational measures or teacher ratings of deviant school behaviors. It is noteworthy that treatment was described as successful based on only a 5% increase in compliance in the home. Furthermore, the treated children did not differ from normal classroom control children in levels of deviant behavior prior to treatment, and noncompliance at school was described as occurring "too infrequently to yield meaningful results." Nevertheless, the researchers noted that five of the eight treated children showed nonsignificant increases in deviant school behavior over the assessment interval, while only four of the eight control children showed similar nonsignificant increases. The authors concluded that further research was required on the contrast effect in parent-child treatment.

In a subsequent study, Breiner and Forehand (1981) obtained school observations and teacher ratings of sixteen children who underwent parent-child treatment for home behavior problems and sixteen same-sex normal classroom control subjects. As in the previously described study, successful completion of treatment was based on relatively small observed behavioral changes: an increase in compliance to parental commands from 30% to 35% and a decrease in oppositional behaviors in the home from 9% to 6%. While these behavioral improvements were statistically significant, it is unclear whether the magnitude of these changes indicates clinically significant behavioral improvement. Also consistent with the previous study, the treatment children did not differ from classroom control children on observational measures or teacher ratings either prior to or after treatment. The authors reasonably concluded that "a contrast effect in the school does not appear to be a concern for parent trainers" (Breiner & Forehand, 1981, p. 40). Unfortunately, the authors extended their interpretation of these results to apply to children exhibiting conduct problem behaviors at school, stating that "If school problems exist, they will not be reduced by treatment directed toward home problems. School problems will have to be directly programmed into an overall treatment package in order to successfully reduce them" (Breiner & Forehand, 1981, p. 41).

In contrast, Cox and Matthews (1977) found lower levels of classroom conduct problems relative to untreated control children based on behavioral observations at the end of a parent training program focusing on family relationships and management skills. These apparent improvements were maintained at a two-month followup. Unfortunately, this study failed to obtain pretreatment evaluations, making it impossible to determine whether the treatment children's favorable comparisons with untreated controls were due to the effects of treatment or simply represented systematic differences between the samples prior to treatment.

Sayger and Horne (1987) found positive improvements in school behavior that were maintained at a nine-month followup after parent training using a social learning model of family therapy. However, this study failed to include a control group and only one measure, the Daily Behavior Checklist (Prinz, O'Connor, & Wilson, 1981), was used to assess school behavior change. In another study employing only a rating scale measure to assess school generalization, improvements on the Devereux Elementary School Behavior Rating Scale (Spivack & Swift, 1967) were greater for children whose parents underwent nonbehavioral group counseling addressing their children's school behavior problems than for children who received direct group counseling (Taylor & Hoedt, 1974). Followup evaluation was not included in this report.

Longterm generalization to the school was suggested by a followup of 40 children whose parents received treatment based on Wahler's Oppositional Child Treatment parent training model (Strain et al., 1982). Classroom behavioral observations conducted three- to nine-years following completion of treatment revealed that treatment children did not differ from randomly selected classroom controls in compliance to teacher commands, on-task behavior, or appropriate peer interactions or on teacher ratings on the Walker Problem Behavior Identification Checklist (Walker, 1970). Although the results of this multimodal assessment are interesting, the results cannot be meaningfully interpreted because no report was made of pretreatment classroom evaluation or of treatment outcome.

A recent study compared the effects of parent-child treatment augmented by positive relationship building and verbally encoded interchanges (stories, conversation, dramatic play) to a minimum treatment control group which received a handout on parenting skills and two videotapes on PMT (Strayhorn & Weidman, 1989). The treated children, whose parents attended an average of 12.5 hours of treatment, failed to show improvements on teacher ratings on the Behar Preschool Behavior Questionnaire (PBQ) (Behar & Stringfield, 1974) immediately following treatment, but significant improvements were documented relative to controls in teacher ratings of ADHD symptoms at the one-year followup (Strayhorn & Weidman, 1991). Interestingly, significant improvements on oppositional and aggressive behaviors were not found in this PMT study which targeted 89 children recruited from the community (Strayhorn & Weidman, 1989).

Webster-Stratton and colleagues (1988) reported significant reductions in teacher-reported behavior problems on the PBQ following parent training programs involving group discussion and combined group discussion with videotape modeling, but actual school behavior was not directly assessed. A more recent study replicated improvements on teacher PBQ ratings at posttreatment, but the gains were not maintained relative to pretreatment scores at a one-year followup (Webster-Stratton & Hammond, 1990).

Parent training was compared with self-control therapy and the combination of the two treatments in a sample of elementary school children with ADHD (Horn, Ialongo, Greenberg, Packard, & Smith-Winberry, 1990). A control group of non-ADHD children was included, but they were not matched for gender or classroom. Improvements were noted at posttreatment for all treatment modalities on teacher ratings on the Conners Teacher Rating Scale (Goyette, Conners, & Ulrich, 1978) and the Teacher Self-Control Rating Scale (Kendall & Wilcox, 1979), but these were not maintained at the eight-month followup.

An extensive two-year treatment that combined parent training with training in social skills, fantasy play and appropriate television viewing was compared to an attention control and a no treatment control in a large French Canadian sample (Tremblay et al., 1991). Subjects were selected on the basis of teacher ratings of disruptive behavior above the 70th percentile in an epidemiological sample. No success was noted on teacher ratings at the end of treatment or on followups one and two years posttreatment.

The studies reviewed provide mixed results on school generalization. The Tremblay et al. (1991) report is not readily comparable to the other PMT treatments reviewed because of the long duration of treatment, the subject selection procedures, and the unusual added elements of treatment (e.g., fantasy play intervention). Of the remaining studies, several of the earlier reports did not find school generalization (e.g., Johnson et al., 1976; Forehand et al., 1979; Breiner & Forehand, 1981). The likelihood of school generalization was diminished in those studies by failure to demonstrate clinically significant behavioral improvement in the home environment and failure to identify an adequate classroom control group. Several other studies reported apparent improvements in classroom behavior following PMT, but failed to document treatment effects clearly (Cox & Matthews, 1977; Strain et al., 1982; Strayhorn & Weidman, 1989) or lacked a control group (Sayger & Horne, 1987; Webster-Stratton & Hammond, 1990). In a controlled study of a referred sample of elementary-aged children, improvements on teacher ratings were noted following treatment, but these improvements were not maintained relative to pretreatment scores at the eight-month followup (Horn et al., 1990).

Most of the studies discussed above relied exclusively on teacher rating scale measures. It is true that teacher ratings have demonstrated high stability for up to four years, despite transitions between classes, schools, and teachers, and that aggressive and externalizing behaviors show the greatest consistency (Verhulst & Van Der Ende,

1991). Campbell has also commented on the impressive stability of teachers' report despite their relatively brief history with the rated children (Campbell & Ewing, 1990). It would appear that teacher ratings are capturing characteristics of students that endure across time and specific environment.

While teacher ratings are an important component of multimodal assessment, previous studies have suggested that treatment effects may be more readily attained on rating scale measures than with measures such as behavioral observations (Eyberg & Johnson, 1974; Johnson & Christensen, 1975). In their review of the parent-child treatment literature, Forehand and Atkeson (1977, p. 575) concluded that "the more rigorous the method of assessment, the less positive the results."

PCIT School Generalization

McNeil et al. (1991) attempted to clarify the conflicting findings on school generalization in a study which corrected some of the methodological problems of previous studies of PMT school generalization. A sample of ten children, referred for significant behavior problems both at home and at school, was evaluated using behavioral observations as well as teacher rating scales to assess school behavior. Pretreatment school assessment revealed that, compared to normal control children, the treatment children showed significantly higher rates of noncompliance, oppositional behavior, and off-task behavior in the classroom as well as elevations on teacher ratings of conduct problem behaviors on the Revised Conners Teacher Rating Scale (Goyette et al., 1978) and the Sutter-Eyberg Student Behavior Inventory (Sutter & Eyberg, 1984). For treatment to be considered successful, children were required to move to within normal limits on a behavioral observation of compliance to parental commands in the clinic (Robinson & Eyberg, 1981) or on the Eyberg Child Behavior Inventory (Eyberg & Ross, 1978; Robinson, Eyberg, & Ross, 1981), a rating scale of home behavior problems. Observed compliance to parental commands for the ten children increased from 40.7% at pretreatment to 70.4% at posttreatment, and Eyberg Child Behavior Inventory pretreatment elevations (Intensity Score: 180.7; Problem Score: 23.3) decreased to within normal limits (Intensity Score: 105.9; Problem Score: 6.1).

Following the completion of treatment, significant improvements on school behavioral observation measures of oppositional behavior and compliance were noted relative to normal control children and nonreferred deviant control subjects within the treated children's classrooms. At the end of treatment, the treatment group fell within one-half standard deviation of the normal control group on the observational measures of compliance and appropriate behavior. In addition, teacher ratings for the treated children improved to within published normal limits on the Conduct Problem factor of the Revised Conners Teacher Rating Scale and on both scales of the Sutter-Eyberg Student Behavior Inventory at posttreatment. In contrast, behavioral observations of on-task behavior and teacher ratings on the Hyperactivity Index of the Revised Conners Teacher Rating Scale, while showing significant improvement relative to pretreatment scores, did not improve significantly more than the deviant control group. Examination of individual children's data indicated that all 10 children improved 30% or more over baseline levels on between 1 and 7 of the 7 outcome measures. Although 3 children showed only minimal improvement (e.g., only 3 of 7 outcome measures showed 30% improvement), there was no evidence of a behavioral contrast effect of worsening classroom behavior following parent-child treatment that some previous studies had suggested.

Discussing differences between this demonstration of school generalization following PCIT, and previous parent-child treatment studies which did not show generalization, the authors noted several features which differed from some previous studies. These differences included 1) demonstration of clinically significant improvements in home behavior, 2) documentation of significant school behavior problems prior to intervention, 3) longer treatment duration (14 sessions) than previous studies (Breiner & Forehand = 8 sessions; Forehand et al. = 9.5 sessions), and 4) use of younger subjects. The age range of children in the McNeil et al. study was 2.6 years to 6.6 years (mean age 4.5), while previous studies included slightly older children.

Treatment Maintenance Research Methodology

Use of Multiple Measures

The importance of using multiple measures at followup, including dependent measures comparable to those employed immediately after treatment, has been noted by a number of investigators (Kendall, Lerner, & Craighead, 1984; Mash & Terdal, 1977; Walker & Hops, 1976). The majority of treatment followup studies have relied on single measures such as a rating scale or an unstructured telephone interview (Mash & Terdal, 1977). In followup assessment, just as at posttreatment assessment, more confidence can be placed in treatment effects that are demonstrated across measurement methods.

Selection of Appropriate Comparison Group

The comparison group used by Strain and colleagues (1982) consisted of four randomly selected classmates of the same age and gender as the treated child. Other investigators have also suggested that classroom peers

provide an appropriate standard for evaluation of
maintenance of school generalization (Kendall, Lerner, &
Craighead, 1984; Walker & Hops, 1976). Walker and Hops
(1976, pp. 159-160) noted that observational data on the
peers of a treated child "can be used to determine normal
limits . . . and can provide a measure of uncontrolled
situational variables that may affect the target subject's
behavior." Kendall and Grove (1988, p. 150) describe
observation of nontreated children in the treatment child's
classroom as the method of choice for behavioral assessment
of classroom interventions, noting that "it is particularly
important that the normal samples come from situations
identical to those of the treated sample." Campbell and
Ewing (1990) compensated for control subject attrition in
their longitudinal study by recruiting new comparison
children from the current classrooms of study children.

In the McNeil et al. study (1991), rather than randomly
selecting classroom controls, normal and deviant control
children were chosen from the classrooms of the treated
children. A deviant control subject (a nonreferred child
identified by school personnel other than the rating teacher
as displaying school behavior problems) was used to serve
the function of an untreated control subject. A normal
control subject (a child described as showing "average"
school behaviors) provided a normative comparison against

which to evaluate the clinical significance of treatment.
This yielded more precision for the labor intensive
classroom observations than relying on random selection of
control children. The children nominated as "average"
controls appeared to be somewhat "better than average" on
teacher rating scale measures, with scores more than a
standard deviation below published norms on the Sutter-
Eyberg Student Behavior Inventory. However, on an
observational measure of compliance, the "average" control
children complied with 73% of teachers' commands, which is
quite close to the 77% average compliance with teacher
commands previously reported as typical for nonreferred
preschoolers (Atwater & Morris, 1988).

Statement of Purpose

The purpose of the present study was to evaluate the
maintenance of school generalization demonstrated by McNeil,
et al. (1991) by evaluating the original subjects twelve
months and eighteen months after completion of Parent-Child
Interaction Therapy. To validly assess the maintenance of
school improvements noted by McNeil et al., methods of
measurement were applied that were comparable to those used
in the original study, and normative comparisons were drawn
from the current peer groups of the treated children.

Followup assessments were in most cases conducted in
new classrooms, with different teachers and classmates from

the classroom in which generalization was previously demonstrated. Treatment children's maintenance of behavioral improvements was measured through comparison with pre- and posttreatment data. The clinical significance of treatment effects was evaluated by comparing the behavior of the treatment children with that of current classmates.

In a modification of previous methodology (McNeil et al., 1991), in which one normal control and one deviant control child were selected, three comparison children were selected from the classroom of each treated child. Students were ranked by teachers as presenting few, average, or many classroom behavior problems, and comparison children were selected to represent this range. Behavioral observations of these control children were used to gauge the maintenance of behavioral effects in treated children. Treated children were also contrasted with comparison children on teacher rating scale measures of conduct problem behaviors, hyperactivity, and social competence.

Hypotheses

1. Treated children will maintain increased levels of appropriate behavior and compliance to teacher's commands over their pretreatment baselines.

2. Treatment children will fall within current classroom norms on the same measures that previously improved to within normal limits. These include percentage

of appropriate behavior and level of compliance during behavioral observations, and teacher ratings on the Revised Conners Teacher Rating Scale and the Sutter-Eyberg Student Behavior Inventory.

3. Percentage of on-task behavior did not show significant improvements during treatment, and there is no reason to expect that it would fall within normal limits at follow-up. On-Task behavior is expected to fall within the pretreatment range and to be comparable to that of the "most behavior problems" comparison group.

4. It is hypothesized that longterm maintenance of increased levels of appropriate behavior and compliance seen at posttreatment will result in social skills ratings that are within normal limits by the time of followup, despite the fact that improvements were not significant relative to controls at posttreatment. Treatment children are expected to show improvement beyond posttreatment levels of social competence and to fall within the range of "average" comparison children at followup.

CHAPTER 2
METHOD

Subjects

Treated Subjects

Subjects in the original school generalization study
and the presently reported followup study comprised a subset
of subjects who participated in a larger treatment outcome
study evaluating Parent-Child Interaction Therapy (PCIT).
Subjects in the PCIT treatment outcome study were children
between the ages of 2 and 7 referred by physicians, mental
health professionals, or school personnel for treatment of
conduct problem behaviors at home and/or at school.

Inclusion criteria for a parent-child dyad in the PCIT
treatment study were as follows: 1) one parent's ratings of
the child's behavior above the published cut-off scores
(i.e., Intensity score = 127, Problem score = 11) on the
Eyberg Child Behavior Inventory (ECBI) (Eyberg & Ross,
1978); 2) designation of Oppositional Defiant Disorder,
Attention-deficit Hyperactivity Disorder, or Conduct
Disorder based on a structured interview with the parent(s);
3) ratio of compliance with parental commands lower than the
average for nonreferred children (i.e., below 62%) in clinic
behavioral observations using the Dyadic Parent-Child
Interaction Coding System (DPICS) (Robinson & Eyberg, 1981);

and 4) no evidence of moderate to severe mental retardation in either the primary caretaker or the child.

A subset of children who met these criteria additionally qualified for inclusion in the original school generalization study by receiving teacher ratings at least one standard deviation above published normal limits on the Conduct Problem factor and/or Hyperactivity Index of the Revised Conners Teacher Rating Scale (Goyette, Conners, & Ulrich, 1976). Twelve children met these criteria for the school generalization study, although only ten were ultimately included in that study. One child was excluded because the school term ended before posttreatment observations could be collected. Another child, who was on medication for treatment of hyperactivity throughout the course of PCIT treatment and followup, was excluded because the research design of the original school generalization study required that subjects not be on medication. All 12 children who met the basic inclusion criteria went on to successfully complete a 14-session course of PCIT with their parent(s), and all 12 were invited to participate in the current study.

Pretreatment results of the DSM-III-R structured interview with parents indicated that, of the original 10 school generalization children, 1 met the criteria for Oppositional Defiant Disorder (ODD), 1 met the criteria for Attention-deficit Hyperactivity Disorder (ADHD), 5 met the criteria for both ODD and ADHD, and 3 children met the criteria for ODD, ADHD, and Conduct Disorder. Regarding the two additional children included in the followup study, both met criteria for ODD and ADHD at pretreatment. McNeil et al. noted that the use of DSM-III-R diagnostic information was provided solely for research sample description because these diagnostic categories have not been validated for children under the age of 7 years old (McNeil et al., 1991).

Although children were not excluded on the basis of gender, race, or SES, all of the children who met the inclusion criteria were male. Eleven of the treatment subjects, including the 2 additional followup subjects, were White, and 1 was of Asian descent. The mean pretreatment age of the original 10 treatment children was 54 months (range = 31 to 79 months). The 2 additional subjects were aged 57 months and 76 months at pretreatment assessment, yielding a mean age of 56 months for the 12 subjects. Six of the treatment children came from two-parent families, and in 4 of these families the father participated in treatment. Four subjects in the original school generalization study, as well as the 2 additional followup subjects, lived with their mother only. On the Four Factor Index of Social Status (Hollingshead, 1975), which ranges from 8 to 66, the mean score for the original 10 subjects was 33.60 ($\underline{SD}$ = 13.49; range = 17 - 61). The mean Hollingshead social status score based on twelve subjects was 36.42 ($\underline{sD}$ = 14.17; range = 17 - 61).

Eleven of the potential 12 subjects (91.67%) participated in the 12-month followup. Of these subjects, incomplete data were collected on 2 children. One teacher provided rating scale measures but refused to allow classroom observations. Another teacher permitted classroom observations, but failed to complete rating scales. Because one subject completed treatment several months later than the other participants in the original school generalization study, this subject's 12-month follow-up assessment occurred concurrently with 18-month follow-up for the other subjects. No 18-month follow-up assessment was conducted for this child, which limited the second followup to eleven subjects. All 11 of these (100%) participated in the full assessment.

The average age at the 12-month followup was 6 years 2 months (range: 3 years 10 months to 7 years 11 months). At the 12-month followup, 3 children were in preschool classrooms, 4 were in kindergarten, 2 were in first grade, and 2 were in second grade. The average age at the 18-month followup was 6 years 8 months (range: 4 years 6 months to 8 years 7 months). At the second followup, 1 child was in preschool, 3 were in kindergarten, 4 were in first grade, 1 was in second grade, and 2 were in third grade.

Eleven of the 12 treatment families remained in the same family constellation at both followups as during treatment (5 two-parent homes and 6 single mothers). In one family the parents had separated prior to the 12-month follow-up, changing the family constellation from a two-parent home to a household headed by a single mother for both followup assessments. Another family underwent a temporary marital separation between the two followup assessments.

As mentioned above, 1 treatment child was on medication for hyperactivity throughout treatment and at both followup intervals. Two children were taking medication for hyperactivity at both the 12-month and 18-month followups. Two additional children, 1 who only participated in the 12-month followup, and 1 who only participated in the 18-month followup, were also placed on stimulant medication following the end of PCIT treatment. Teachers were asked if any of the children showed atypical behavior during the observations. At the first observation period, one teacher noted that a treatment child had recently been placed on medication and appeared calmer than usual. A comparison child in a different classroom was described as more difficult than usual due to the recent birth of a sibling. At the 18-month followup, 1 treatment child left school early due to a cold following observations on one of the three days he was observed. Another teacher reported that she changed her behavior toward a treatment child during the observations by giving "many more cues than usual" and extending his task times to longer than she typically required.

Four treatment children were receiving special educational services at the time of the 12-month followup.

Two of these were originally referred by a developmental preschool where they were enrolled throughout the course of PCIT treatment. One of these children remained in the developmental preschool at first followup, while the second had moved to a special education kindergarten classroom. A third target child was in an ESE (Exceptional Student Education) placement, and another had been referred for special services for learning disabilities (LD) in his regular first grade at the 12-month followup.

Six of the 11 target children were receiving special educational services at the time of the 18-month followup. One child had moved from developmental preschool into a self-contained multi-handicapped primary school classroom. The other child from developmental preschool had been mainstreamed into a regular kindergarten with ongoing special services. The 2 children receiving, respectively, ESE and LD services at the first observation continued in these placements. Finally, 2 additional children had been referred for LD services at the second followup interval.

Comparison Subjects

Three comparison subjects were chosen from the classroom of each treatment subject at each followup interval. Passive consent forms (see Appendix A) were sent home to all children in each treatment child's class a minimum of one week prior to observations. Parents who did not want their child to participate responded by signing the form and returning it to the teacher. Two or fewer refusals were received in each classroom, with no refusals in most.

For selection of comparison children, the teacher of the target child's class was asked to list (by initials) all boys in her classroom, omitting any whose parents had declined participation. Children differing in age from the target child by more than one year were also deleted from the list of potential comparison subjects, as were those who were nonverbal, blind, or nonambulatory. The teacher then rated each child on a 1-5 scale where "1" represented "the fewest problems relative to the behavior of boys in this class" and "5" represented "the most behavior problems relative to the behavior of boys in this class" (see Appendix B). Three comparison subjects were then selected to be observed along with the treated child, one rated as "1," one rated as "3," and one rated as "5."

In cases where more than one child received the same rating (e.g. "3"), the comparison child was chosen randomly from the available subjects. In cases where no child was available for observation with a given rating (e.g., child rated "5" was absent), a child receiving the nearest numerical rating (e.g., "4") was selected at random as the comparison subject. If no child with a "3" rating was eligible, a comparison child was randomly selected from those receiving ratings of "2" and "4". At the 12-month followup, the mean rating of comparison children with fewest behavior problems was 1.09 across the 11 classrooms. The mean rating for comparison children with "average" behavior problems was 2.82, and the mean rating for comparison children with most behavior problems was 4.64. At the 18-month followup, the mean rating of comparison children with fewest behavior problems was 1.00 across the 11 classrooms. The mean rating for comparison children with "average" behavior problems was 3.00, and the mean rating for comparison children with most behavior problems was 4.54.

At each followup interval teachers were asked whether they felt any of the children they rated were in need of treatment for behavior problems. At the 12-month followup, 3 treatment children, 6 "most behavior problems" comparison children and 1 "average behavior" comparison child were judged to need treatment. At the 18-month followup, 4 target children, 7 "most behavior problems" comparison children and 1 "average behavior" comparison child were identified as in need of treatment. Seven of the 33 comparison children (21%) were receiving special educational services at the 12-month followup; these included 2 "few problems" comparison children, 2 "average problems" comparison children, and 3 "most behavior problems" comparison children. Nine of 33 comparison subjects (27%) were receiving special educational services at the 18-month followup; 1 "few problems" comparison child, 3 "average problems" comparison children, and 5 "most behavior problems" comparison children.

As mentioned above, comparison children with an age difference of more than one year from the treatment child were excluded where possible. An exception was made at the 18-month followup, when 1 treatment subject had been placed in a primary school ESE classroom where he was more than two years younger than his classmates. In that classroom, comparison children were matched for mental age within 2 years of the treated child, based on the teacher's report.

Comparison children, matched for gender to treatment subjects, were all male. Age was not recorded for all comparison children, but for the 80% (53 out of 66) for whom age was reported, ages of comparison subjects ranged from 3 years, 5 months to 8 years, 9 months at the first followup and from 4 years (months not reported) to 11 years, 7 months at the second followup.

Measures

Eyberg Child Behavior Inventory (ECBI)

The ECBI is a brief, psychometrically sound measure of disruptive behaviors of children aged 2 to 16 (Eyberg, 1992). The ECBI provides a list of 36 conduct problem behaviors, including items such as "sasses adults," "whines," "physically fights with brothers and sisters," and "is overactive or restless" (see Appendix C). Each behavior is rated on two dimensions, frequency of occurrence and identification as a problem. Parents indicate how often the behavior currently occurs on a scale from "never" (1) to "always" (7), and the item ratings are summed to yield the intensity score which has a potential range of 36 to 252. Parents also indicate whether the behavior is currently a problem on a yes/no scale, yielding a problem score which is the sum of "yes" responses and has a potential range of 0 to 36.

The ECBI was initially standardized on preschool samples (age range: 2 to 7 years) of 42 normal children and 43 behavior problem children (Eyberg & Ross, 1978). The normal preschoolers had a mean intensity score of 102.6 (S.D. = 25.5) and a mean problem score of 4.62 (S.D. = 8.8). Subsequent studies expanded standardization of the ECBI throughout the targeted age range of 2 through 16 years and established the psychometric properties of the instrument (Boggs, Eyberg, & Reynolds, 1990; Eyberg & Robinson, 1983; Robinson, Eyberg, & Ross, 1980). Internal consistency coefficients of .98 have been reported for both scales of the ECBI, and test-retest stability over a 3-week period has been found satisfactory for both the Intensity Scale (r = .86) and the Problem Scale (r = .88) (Robinson et al., 1980). Subsequent reports have demonstrated that ECBI scores are stable over repeated administrations (Eyberg & Boggs, 1989) and over intervals of up to one year (Pearson's correlation: $r(32)$ = .75 for Intensity and Problem scales) (Funderburk, Eyberg, & Behar, 1993).

ECBI scores have been shown to relate significantly to direct observational measures of parent-child interaction, activity level, and temperament (Robinson & Eyberg, 1981;

Webster-Stratton & Eyberg, 1982) as well as to the Child
Behavior Checklist (CBCL Externalizing total score
correlated .67 with ECBI intensity score and .75 with ECBI
problem score) (Boggs et al., 1990). Several studies have
demonstrated discrimination among nonreferred, conduct
problem, neglected, and other clinic-referred children
(Argona & Eyberg, 1981; Eyberg & Robinson, 1983; Eyberg &
Ross, 1978; Robinson et al., 1980). Finally, the ECBI has
been shown to be sensitive to treatment effects of parent
training programs (Eisenstadt et al., in press; Eyberg &
Robinson, 1982; Packard, Robinson, & Grove, 1983; Webster-
Stratton, 1982, 1984; Wolfe, Sandler, & Kaufman, 1981).

Revised Conners Teacher Rating Scale (RCTRS)

The RCTRS is a shortened version of the original 39-
item Conners Teacher Rating Scale (Conners, 1969). Both
teacher rating scales were designed to help identify
hyperactive children, although additional symptom patterns
have also been assessed based on factor analysis of the
scales. The RCTRS asks teachers to rate the degree to which
a child exhibits each of 28 listed symptoms on a 4-point
scale ranging from "not at all" (0) to "very much" (3) (see
Appendix D). The revised scale includes three factors:
Conduct Problem, Hyperactivity, and Inattentive-Passive, as
well as a total score which is the average score of the 28
items. Factor scores are obtained by summing the points for
each item on a factor and dividing by the number of items on
that factor.

The RCTRS was standardized on a sample of 570 children between the ages of 3 and 17 (Goyette et al., 1978). Mean factor scores of three- to five-year-olds ($\underline{n}$ = 24) in the normative sample were: Conduct Problem = .49 ($\underline{SD}$ = .74); Hyperactivity = .74 ($\underline{SD}$ = .74); and Inattentive-passive = .83 ($\underline{SD}$ = .87). Mean factor scores for the six- to eight-year-old age range ($\underline{n}$ = 102) were: Conduct Problem = .30 ($\underline{SD}$ = .41); Hyperactivity = .46 ($\underline{SD}$ = .57); and Inattentive-passive = .64 ($\underline{SD}$ = .71).

The factor structure of the RCTRS was shown to be highly congruent with the longer original Conners Teacher Rating Scale (Goyette et al., 1978). The 39-item version of the rating scale has demonstrated stability over a one-month interval (Pearson's correlations of .72 - .91 for the total and factor scores) (Conners, 1969). Stability coefficients of .94 - .98 were found for the total and factor scores of the RCTRS (Edelbrock & Reed, 1984). The RCTRS has shown significant correlations with the Conners Parent Rating Scale, although there are no available reports of interteacher agreement (Goyette et al., 1978). Research on the Conners scales has demonstrated differentiation between normal and hyperactive children and sensitivity to the effects of medication for hyperactivity (Conners, 1970).

Sutter-Eyberg Student Behavior Inventory (SESBI)

The SESBI (Sutter & Eyberg, 1984) was designed as a unidimensional measure of classroom conduct problem behaviors to aid in discriminating normal children from children in need of treatment for school conduct problem behaviors (Eyberg, 1992). The SESBI provides a list of 36 conduct problem behaviors observable by teachers (see Appendix E). It has the same format and scoring as the ECBI, with behaviors rated on two dimensions, frequency of occurrence and identification as a problem.

The SESBI was standardized on a sample of 55 preschoolers aged 3 to 5 in Gainesville, Florida (Funderburk & Eyberg, 1989). The mean intensity score for this sample was 100.9 with a standard deviation of 47.6 and a range of scores from 36 to 228. The mean problem score was 6.0 with a standard deviation of 8.8 and a range of scores from 0 to 33. The SESBI showed acceptable interteacher agreement (mean r = .85 for the Intensity Scale and mean r = .87 for the Problem Scale based on seven and six pairs of teachers, respectively) and high internal consistency coefficients of .98 for the Intensity Scale and .96 for the Problem Scale (Funderburk & Eyberg, 1989). Funderburk and Eyberg (1989) assessed test-retest stability over a 1-week interval, finding coefficients of .90 for the Intensity Scale and .89 for the Problem Scale. Significant correlations have been found between the SESBI and several school rating scales including the Conners Teacher Rating Scale (correlations ranged from .67 to .92 between the two SESBI scales and the Conners Conduct Problem Factor, Hyperactivity Factor, Inattentive/Passive Factor, and Hyperkinesis Factor) (Sosna, Ladish, Warner, & Burns, 1989), the Child Behavior

Checklist--Teacher Form (correlations of .87 and .71 of
SESBI intensity and problem scores with CBC externalizing
score) (Schaughency, Hurley, Yano, Seeley, & Talarico,
1989), and the Behar Preschool Behavior Questionnaire
(correlations of .76 and .61 between the Behar total score
and the SESBI intensity and problem scores, respectively)
(Funderburk & Eyberg, 1989). Significant correlations have
also been found in a sample of behavior problem children
between the SESBI and classroom observational measures of
appropriate behavior (correlations of -.67 and -.70 with the
SESBI intensity and problem scores) and on-task behavior
(correlations of -.54 and -.58 with the SESBI intensity and
problem scores) (Newcomb, Eyberg, Bodiford, Eisenstadt, &
Funderburk, 1989). Initial evidence that the SESBI
discriminates between children referred for school behavior
problems and those referred for developmental problems has
been reported (Funderburk & Eyberg, 1989). Finally, the
original school generalization study demonstrated that the
SESBI is sensitive to treatment effects (McNeil et al.,
1991).

Walker-McConnell Scale of Social Competence and School
    Adjustment: A Social Skills Rating Scale for Teachers

The Walker-McConnell is a school rating scale designed
to assess adaptive classroom behavior and interpersonal
social competence in elementary-aged school children (Walker
& McConnell, 1987). The scale's 43 items are positively
stated descriptions of social skills which are rated by

teachers on a 1 ("never") to 5 ("frequently") Likert scale
(see Appendix F). The scale yields a total score and scores
on three subscales: 1) Teacher Preferred Social Behavior,
defined as "peer related social behavior that is highly
valued or preferred by teachers;" 2) Peer Preferred Social
Behavior, defined as "peer related social behavior that is
highly valued by peers;" and 3) School Adjustment Behavior,
defined as "social-behavioral competencies that are highly
valued by teachers within classroom instructional contexts."

The Walker-McConnell was standardized on a national
normative sample of 1812 elementary school children. Mean
scores for the normative sample were as follows: Total Scale
= 161.35 ($\underline{SD}$ = 32.41); Teacher-Preferred Social Behavior =
58.74 ($\underline{SD}$ = 13.51); Peer-Preferred Social Behavior = 63.72
($\underline{SD}$ = 13.05); and School Adjustment Behavior = 38.90 ($\underline{SD}$ =
9.74). Internal consistency coefficients of .97, .96, .95,
and .96 were found for the Total Scale and three subscales,
respectively. Low to moderate interrater agreement has been
reported for small samples, with higher agreement reported
for nonclinical samples (Total Scale = .77; subscales = .63-
.83) than for a clinical sample (Total Scale = .53;
subscales = .36 - .52) (Walker & McConnell, 1987). Hops
(1987) evaluated test-retest stability over a three-week
interval for 323 second and fourth graders. Test-retest
coefficients were .90, .88, and .92 for the three subscales.
Long-term test-retest stability was investigated over the
interval from fall to spring of the academic year for a

"sample of 80 antisocial and normal pupils in the fifth and sixth grades" (Walker & McConnell, 1987). Test-retest correlations over this interval were .67, .61, .70, and .65, respectively, for the total scale and subscales 1 - 3.

Classroom Observational Coding System

The classroom behavioral coding system used in the current study represents a modified version of that used in the original school generalization study (McNeil et al., 1991). Like in the McNeil et al. study, three behavior categories were coded: 1) appropriate vs. oppositional behavior vs. unsure; 2) comply vs. noncomply vs. unsure/no command; and 3) on task vs. off task vs. not applicable. This coding system combined procedures used by the Forehand research group (Breiner & Forehand, 1981; Forehand, Sturgis, McMahon, Aguar, Green, & Breiner, 1979) with procedures used by Walker and colleagues (Walker, Shinn, O'Neill, & Ramsey, 1987). The categories of appropriate vs. oppositional and compliant vs. noncompliant behavior were used in previous studies of generalization of parent-child therapy to the school setting (Breiner & Forehand, 1981; Forehand et al., 1979). The Forehand group's studies did not include a measure of on-task behavior. Walker et al. (1987) defined the on-task category used here as "academically engaged time." Definitions of the school behavior coding categories used in the original school generalization study are presented in Appendix G. These same definitions were maintained in the followup study, with some modifications to

promote clarity. The revised school behavioral definitions
are presented in Appendix H.

The time-sampling procedure used by McNeil et al.
(1991) was similar to that employed by the Forehand group.
McNeil et al. used 10-second observation intervals followed
by 10-second intervals for recording, whereas the previous
school generalization studies used 10-second observation
intervals followed by 5-second recording intervals (Breiner
& Forehand, 1981; Forehand et al., 1979). Walker et al.
(1987) originally recorded the duration of academically
engaged time rather than using time-sampling for this
category. The McNeil et al. category of on-task behavior
maintained Walker's definition, but coded on-task behavior
in 10-second intervals. For on-task to be coded,
academically engaged behavior was required throughout the
10-second interval; off-task would be coded for that
interval if any nonengaged time occurred. A similar
modified time-sampling procedure, combining frequency coding
of oppositional behaviors and compliance with modified
duration coding of on-task behavior, has been used in other
well-researched school behavioral coding systems for
hyperactive children (Abikoff, Gittelman, & Klein, 1980;
Abikoff, Gittelman-Klein, & Klein, 1977).

McNeil et al. (1991) found high percentages of
agreement among coders: appropriate = 92.6% (range: 87% -
97%); comply = 93.2% (range: 83% - 99%); and on task = 90.0%
(range: 80% - 96%). These interrater agreement statistics

are similar to those, all above 90%, reported by Forehand and colleagues and Walker and colleagues for their versions of the coding system (Forehand et al., 1979; Walker et al., 1907).

In the McNeil et al. (1991) coding system the target child and two control children were each observed for 10 seconds out of every minute, and 45 minutes were coded during each observation period, yielding seven and one half minutes of data per child. Two observation periods were included in each assessment, yielding approximately 15 minutes of data per child.

Because the present study included an additional comparison subject, a more efficient sampling procedure was desired. The alternative procedure consisted of consecutive 10-second intervals for one minute with a 15-second break after each minute. This type of behavioral coding also has been described in previously reported school observation systems (Abikoff et al., 1980; Strain, Steele, Ellis, & Timm, 1982; Walker & Hops, 1976). The method allows four children to be coded for two minutes each in a 10-minute cycle. Five observation cycles were coded in each observation period, providing 10 minutes of data for each subject. Three observation periods were included in each assessment, yielding approximately 30 minutes of data per child at each followup interval.

Observation sessions were conducted on three different days within ten consecutive school days whenever possible.

This 10-day interval was exceeded in three cases at the 12-month followup assessment due to 1 target child unexpectedly leaving town for several weeks (interval of data collection = 29 days), and two classrooms having extensive absences due to chicken pox (intervals of 24 and 47 days for data collection). It was not possible to complete three days of observation in two of the target classrooms at the 12-month followup due to the approaching end of the school year. Two days of observations were completed in one of these classrooms and one day of observations in the other. These observation periods were extended for longer than standard to approximate the goal of 30 minutes of data per child. Twenty-nine minutes of coding were achieved for the treated child and comparison children available on two observation days, and 20 minutes of coding were achieved for the treated child and comparison children available for only one day. Observations were rescheduled if a treated child was absent, but occasionally comparison children were also absent, thereby reducing the available data for some comparison children. Fewer than 30 minutes of data were coded on 5 of the 66 comparison subjects (3 "fewest problems," 1 "average problems," and 1 "most problems" comparison child); data collected ranged from 10 to 24 minutes for these comparison children.

Observations were conducted within a 10-school-day period in each classroom at the 18-month followup assessment, and 3 days of observation were attained for 9 of the 11 treatment children. Only 2 days of observation were possible in the two remaining classrooms. Fewer than 30 minutes of data were coded for one target child (24 minutes), one "fewest problems" comparison child (24 minutes), two "average problems" comparison children (15 and 20 minutes), and two "most problems" comparison children (12 and 24 minutes).

The school coding system yields a percentage score for each of the three behavior categories: appropriate behavior, time on task, and compliance. The percentage of appropriate behavior was derived from the intervals in which appropriate behavior was coded divided by the total number of intervals. Percentage of time on task was calculated as the total intervals of on-task behavior divided by the total of on-task plus off-task intervals, omitting intervals in which the category was not applicable. Percent compliance represents the total number of commands obeyed divided by the total number of commands directed toward the child.

Interrater agreement percentages, defined as the number of agreements divided by the number of agreements plus disagreements, were calculated in the present study to conform with the method used in the original school generalization study. Kappa statistics of interrater agreement were also calculated in order to control for chance agreements. Kappa and percent agreement scores were computed for each of the three behavior categories: appropriate behavior, compliance, and on-task behavior.

Procedures

Classroom Evaluation

Parents of children who completed the school generalization study (McNeil et al., 1991) completed a followup contact form at the end of treatment in which they provided permission to be contacted for followup along with addresses and telephone numbers (see Appendix I). Parents were contacted with a description of the school generalization followup by telephone, mail, or in person during followup assessments at the psychology clinic scheduled as part of a separate research project. All agreed to participate and signed an informed consent (see Appendix J) and a release of information permitting communication with the child's school (see Appendix K).

Parents who returned for research assessments at the psychology clinic within one month of scheduled school observations completed ECBIs during their clinic visit. Other parents were mailed ECBIs along with return postage. Parents who failed to return an ECBI after two mailings were contacted by telephone when possible and read the ECBI over the telephone.

Once parental consent was obtained, the teacher and/or principal of each treated child's school were contacted by telephone and provided with a description of the research. The various participating schools varied in their requirements for approval of research projects. Procedures ranged from simply scheduling visits with the teacher to providing information to a school board for review to submitting a standardized research application to a county public school system's research director. Principals were provided with a copy of the parent's information release for the school's records. At the time of initial contact the teacher was questioned as to his/her knowledge of the identity of the treated child. In cases where the teacher was unaware of which child had received treatment, he or she was not informed prior to the assessment in order to elicit blind ratings. Despite these efforts, most teachers were aware (generally through parent-teacher conferences or conversation with previous teachers) of the treated child's status. Four of 11 teachers were blind to treatment status at the 12-month followup and 3 of 11 were blind at the 18-month followup.

Once approval was obtained to collect data, the teacher was consulted (usually by telephone) to schedule three days of observation during relatively structured classroom activity times. These times were selected as those when teachers were likely to place most demands on students, because previous school generalization studies (Forehand et al., 1979) reported difficulty obtaining a high enough rate of commands to reliably code compliance. Letters containing passive consent forms for comparison children (see Appendix A) were given to the teacher to be sent home with every child in the class a minimum of five school days prior to observations.

On the first scheduled observation day, once the experimenter selected the comparison children on the basis of the teacher's 1-5 rankings, the children to be observed were pointed out, when possible, by someone other than the teacher (e.g., the classroom aide). In cases where no one else was present to identify the children, the teacher was asked to point out several additional children so as to minimize the likelihood that the teacher would know specifically which children were being observed. The teacher was told that, in addition to the treated child, a cross-section of children were randomly chosen to represent the range of behavior in the classroom.

Behavioral observations were collected from an unobtrusive location in the classroom according to the procedure described in the section on the Classroom Coding System. On the final day of observations, the teacher was given rating forms to complete on the treated child and comparison children. The teacher was asked to complete the RCTRS, the SESBI, and the Walker-McConnell on the four children. The teacher also completed a form noting whether the children's behavior was typical during the observations and whether any of the children, to the teacher's knowledge, were receiving or in need of special education services or treatment for behavior problems (see Appendix L). Upon completion of the rating scales the teacher was reimbursed $20 for his or her time.

One treatment child remained in the same classroom and with the same teacher at first followup as during treatment. The other ten participants in the 12-month followup were in different classrooms. All 18-month followup assessments occurred in different classrooms from 12-month observations. The same procedure was followed for each follow-up assessment, including the comparison subject selection process. No attempt was made to track comparison children from the 12-month to 18-month followup since they were never identified by name.

Interrater Reliability Calculations and Coder Training

Primary coders were five graduate students and one advanced undergraduate research assistant who were blind to the treatment status of the children. Coders who collected 12-month observations did not code the same treated child at the 18-month observation. The experimenter served as a reliability coder and accompanied the primary coder for 67% of observations (62% at the 12-month followup and 71% at the 18-month followup). When two coders were present, they coded simultaneously using a dual-jack earphone for the taped interval signals. The reliability coder's data were used only in reliability calculations; the data of the primary coder who was blind to treatment status were always used in data analysis.

Reliability was calculated by two methods. Percent agreement was used to replicate reliability results from McNeil et al. (1991), and the Kappa statistic was used to control for chance agreement. The Appropriate behavior variable was calculated first in terms of agreement on specific misbehaviors (e.g., no agreement coded if primary coder noted "disruptive" and the reliability coder noted "out of seat") and then by collapsing categories of misbehavior into a global agreement on the presence or absence of inappropriate behaviors. The overall percent agreement for appropriate behavior was .89 for global agreement and .85 for specific agreement. Kappa statistics for appropriate behavior were .56 for global agreement and .59 for specific agreement. For the compliance variable, overall percent agreement was .83 and Kappa was .65. For the on-task variable, overall percent agreement was .88 and Kappa was .66. Table 1 presents overall reliability statistics as well as reliabilities calculated per followup, per coder, and per subject.

Coder training consisted of didactic presentations, practice coding of videotapes of children in dyadic interactions with parents and in classroom situations, and live classroom coding in a laboratory preschool. Coders were required to attain an 80% reliability criterion in a 90-minute live coding session before collecting data for the study. Regular training sessions employing didactic presentations and coding of videotapes were used to reduce the possibility of observer drift. Training time required to meet the criterion ranged from 5.5 hours for a graduate student with extensive prior experience with the Dyadic

Parent-Child Interaction Coding System to 24.5 hours for an advanced undergraduate student with little prior behavioral coding experience. The average total training time for graduate student coders was 9.2 hours with an average of 1.4 hours of didactic training, 1.3 hours of coding from videotapes, and 6.5 hours of live coding. As mentioned above, 24.5 total hours of training were required for the one undergraduate coder; these included 5 hours of didactic training, 5.5 hours of coding videotapes, and 14 hours of live coding.

Table 1

Interrater Agreement Results

| | APPROPRIATE | | COMPLIANCE | ON TASK |
| | Global | Specific | | |
	% Agree/Kappa	% Agree/Kappa	%Agree/Kappa	%Agree/Kappa
Overall				
Total	.89/.56	.85/.59	.83/.65	.88/.66
12-Month	.92/.63	.88/.61	.85/.69	.90/.68
18-Month	.87/.52	.83/.58	.80/.59	.86/.64
By Coder				
Coder 1	.93/.58	.91/.60	.86/.74	.90/.70
Coder 2	.88/.55	.84/.58	.81/.58	.88/.68
Coder 3	.92/.63	.88/.61	.89/.68	.91/.71
Coder 4	.87/.46	.83/.55	.72/.52	.80/.49
Coder 5	.92/.64	.89/.64	.90/.78	.94/.75
Coder 6	.91/.68	.82/.59	.83/.49	.87/.61
By Subject - 12-Month Followup[a]				
Sub. 1	.86/.54	.78/.53	.90/.80	.86/.73
Sub. 2	.94/.68	.92/.70	.89/.78	.96/.75
Sub. 3	.91/.62	.84/.59	.83/.56	.86/.58
Sub. 6	.94/.63	.91/.64	.88/.78	.91/.72
Sub. 7	.92/.69	.86/.61	1.0/---	.95/.82
Sub. 8	.90/.68	.81/.59	.83/.54	.86/.61
Sub. 9	.93/.61	.89/.59	.86/.58	.90/.67
Sub. 12	.91/.38	.90/.56	.63/.36	.89/.61

Table 1--continued

	APPROPRIATE		COMPLIANCE	ON TASK
	Global	Specific		
	% Agree/Kappa	% Agree/Kappa	%Agree/Kappa	%Agree/Kappa

By Subject - 18-Month Followup[b]

Sub. 1	.83/.49	.80/.57	.74/.51	.82/.62
Sub. 2	.82/.48	.74/.51	.76/.58	.72/.44
Sub. 3	.92/.69	.90/.70	.88/0.0	.89/.74
Sub. 4	.95/.64	.93/.67	.83/.64	.94/.70
Sub. 5	.84/.50	.78/.54	.88/.65	.85/.60
Sub. 6	.89/.67	.81/.62	.86/.55	.91/.79
Sub. 7	.79/.37	.78/.54	.71/.47	.77/.52
Sub. 9	.82/.38	.79/.53	.85/.73	.93/.79
Sub. 10	.89/.36	.86/.52	.75/.57	.94/.75
Sub. 11	.95/.15	.94/.49	.76/.20	.88/.47

Note. Percent agreement is reported on the left and Kappa
   is reported on the right of the slash mark.
[a] Subject 4 and subject 5 did not participate in the 12-
   month followup classroom observations. Reliability
   coding was not done for subject 10 and subject 11.
[b] Subject 12 did not participate in the 18-month followup
   classroom observations. Reliability coding was not done
   for subject 8.

Treatment Subject Analysis of Variance

Treated children's outcome on dependent variables was evaluated using a one group, repeated measures ANOVA to compare scores across the four assessment intervals: pretreatment, posttreatment, 12-month followup, and 18-month followup. Polynomial contrasts were then used to evaluate the nature of the repeated measures effect, e.g., upward or downward shifts in mean scores across the four time intervals. For example, all variables could be expected to show a linear trend from pretreatment to posttreatment. If this trend continued through both followup intervals, the polynomial contrast would document a simple linear pattern. If, however, scores significantly regressed toward pretreatment levels after the observed posttreatment improvement, then the polynomial contrast would indicate a quadratic trend. A more complex pattern, with more than two statistically significant "bends" in the data, would be indicated by a cubic result in the polynomial contrast. To illustrate the results of the polynomial contrasts, mean scores for each assessment interval were graphed.

Behavioral Observations

Means and standard deviations for the observation variables across the four assessment intervals are shown in

Table 2. Analysis of variance of behavior observation variables revealed significant effects for compliance ($F(3,6) = 5.06$, $p = .04$) and appropriate behavior ($F(3,6) = 11.72$, $p - .006$), but not for on task behavior ($F(3,6) = 2.54$, n.s.). It may be recalled that significant results were not obtained for the on task variable in the original McNeil et al. school generalization study (1991).

Table 2

Mean Scores for Treated Children on Observational Measures of Classroom Behavior Across Time

	Pre-Trt	Post-Trt	Fup 1	Fup 2	
	M	M	M	M	$F(3,6)$
	(SD)	(SD)	(SD)	(SD)	
% Compliance	50.2	85.6	78.8	76.0	5.06[*]
	(27.7)	(18.0)	(15.0)	(17.1)	
% Appropriate	61.9	83.8	86.0	75.1	11.72[**]
	(18.1)	(17.5)	(13.2)	(11.5)	
% On Task	68.0	81.1	79.8	67.7	2.54
	(17.2)	(15.8)	(14.7)	(11.4)	

$N = 9$
[*] $p < .05$ [**] $p < .001$

Figures 1-3 display mean scores for the behavioral observation measures plotted across the four assessment

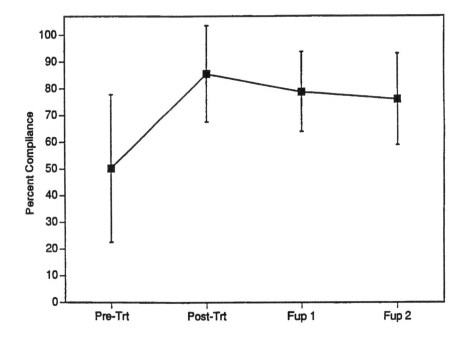

Figure 1. Mean percent compliance for treated children across four assessments, with error bars denoting 1 standard deviation.

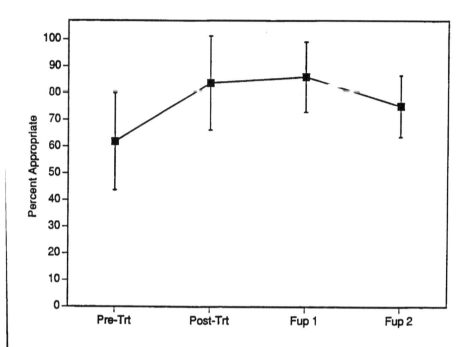

Figure 2. Mean percent appropriate behavior for treated children across four assessments, with error bars denoting 1 standard deviation.

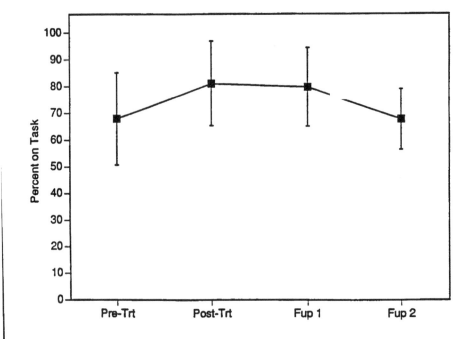

Figure 3. Mean percent on-task behavior for treated
children across four assessments, with error bars denoting 1
standard deviation.

intervals. The compliance variable (see Figure 1) showed a significant linear trend ($\underline{F}(1,8)$ = 6.51, $\underline{p}$ = .03) as well as a significant quadratic trend ($\underline{F}(1,8)$ = 13.99, $\underline{p}$ = .006), documenting the increase in compliance from pretreatment to posttreatment, followed by a downward "bend" in the data as scores declined slightly across follow-ups. Compliance percentages remained within one standard deviation of posttreatment scores at both followup assessments.

Percentages of appropriate behavior also remained within one standard deviation of posttreatment percent appropriate, with even a slight increase between posttreatment and 12-month followup. However, the percent appropriate score at second followup is also within one standard deviation of the pretreatment score, as shown in Table 2. This parabolic shape is confirmed by the significant second degree polynomial contrast ($\underline{F}(1,8)$ = 29.55, p = .0006), or quadratic trend, illustrated in Figure 2.

As mentioned above, the ANOVA results were not significant for the on-task variable. Scores at posttreatment and both followups fall within one standard deviation of pretreatment scores. Percent of on-task behavior at second follow-up dipped slightly below its pretreatment level. To summarize, analyses of behavioral observation measures showed mixed results. On-task behavior showed no significant improvement at posttreatment or across followups. For appropriate behavior, significant posttreatment improvements were maintained at the 12-month followup but not at the 18-month followup. Compliance showed the strongest effect and it was maintained across both followups.

Teacher Ratings

Means and standard deviations across the four assessment intervals are shown in Table 3 for the SESBI scales, and the Conners Hyperactivity Index, Conduct Problem factor, and Inattentive-Passive factor. Analysis of variance revealed significant effects for both the SESBI Intensity scale ($F(3,6) = 5.26$, $p = .04$) and Problem scale ($F(3,6) = 8.44$, $p = .02$), as well as the Conners Conduct Problem factor ($F(3,6) = 12.06$, $p = .006$). Analysis of variance revealed near significant effects for the Conners Hyperactivity Index ($F(3,6) = 4.28$, $p = .06$) and Conners Inattentive-Passive factor ($F(3,6) = 3.58$, $p = .09$). Polynomial contrasts for all of these teacher rating variables showed significant results for the second degree, or quadratic contrast. Polynomial contrast values are shown in Table 4. Figures 4 - 8 illustrate the parabolic curve of the plotted means, with pretreatment to posttreatment decline in rated problems followed by a flat maintenance curve to the 12-month followup, and finally by degeneration toward pretreatment levels at the 18-month follow-up. Mean scores at the 12-month followup were generally equivalent to posttreatment scores, whereas at the 18-month followup, scores fell within one standard deviation of the

pretreatment mean for all teacher ratings examined except
the Conners Conduct Problem factor (See Table 3).

Table 3

Mean Scores for Treated Children on Teacher Ratings of
Classroom Behavior Problems Across Time

	Pre-Trt	Post-Trt	Fup 1	Fup 2	
	M	M	M	M	$F(3,6)$
	(SD)	(SD)	(SD)	(SD)	
SESBI					
Intensity	153.0	108.0	117.3	142.1	5.26*
	(17.8)	(29.2)	(38.1)	(45.0)	
Problem	20.8	8.0	9.3	14.9	8.44**
	(6.0)	(5.9)	(8.5)	(9.4)	
Revised Conners					
Hyper. Index	2.0	1.3	1.4	1.9	4.28
	(.63)	(.72)	(.79)	(.89)	
Conduct Probs.	1.61	.84	.99	1.08	12.06**
	(.33)	(.47)	(.59)	(.67)	
Inatt. Passive	1.51	.97	1.30	1.67	3.58
	(.73)	(.71)	(.94)	(.79)	

$N = 9$
* $p < .05$ ** $p < .01$

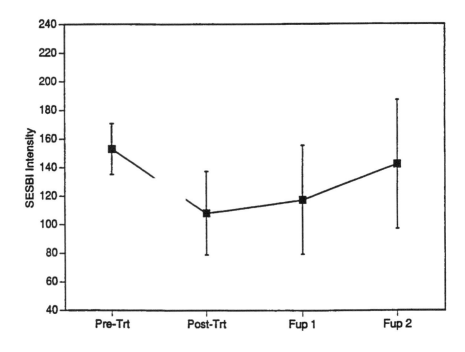

Figure 4. Mean SESBI Intensity Scores for treated children across four assessments, with error bars denoting 1 standard deviation.

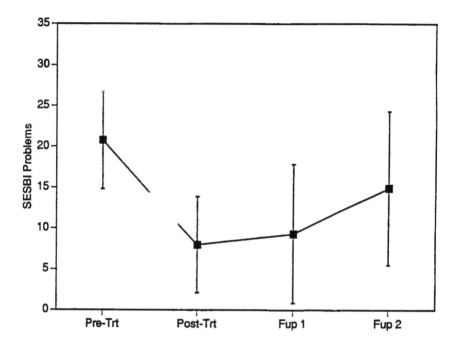

Figure 5. Mean SESBI Problem Scores for treated children across four assessments, with error bars denoting 1 standard deviation.

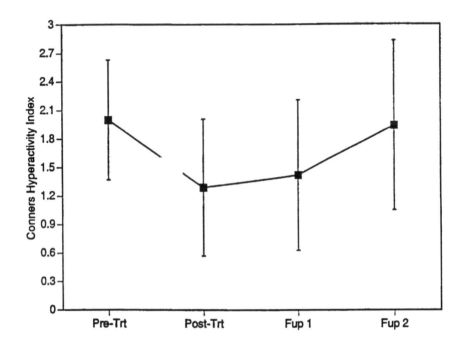

Figure 6. Mean RCTRS Hyperactivity Index scores for treated children across four assessments, with error bars denoting 1 standard deviation.

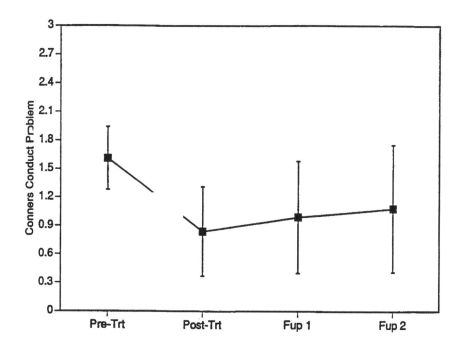

Figure 7. Mean RCTRS Conduct Problem factor scores for treated children across four assessments, with error bars denoting 1 standard deviation.

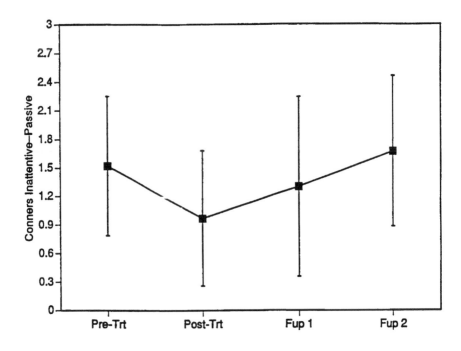

<u>Figure 8</u>. Mean RCTRS Inattentive-Passive factor scores for treated children across four assessments, with error bars denoting 1 standard deviation.

	Polynomial Contrast Values		
	1st Degree	2nd Degree	3rd Degree
	F(1,8) p	F(1,8) p	F(1,8) p
SESBI			
Intensity	0.18 n.s	16.41 .004	1.31 n.s.
Problem	3.37 n.s.	19.74 .002	1.56 n.s.
Revised Conners			
Hyper. Index	0.00 n.s.	14.64 .005	0.38 n.s.
Conduct Probs.	3.68 n.s.	12.74 .007	1.59 n.s.
Inatt. Passive	0.77 n.s.	5.86 .042	1.64 n.s.

$\underline{N} = 9$

Social Skills Ratings

Means and standard deviations are shown in Table 5 for the Walker-McConnell total and subscale scores across the four assessment intervals. Higher scores represent greater social competence on this measure. Analysis of variance revealed significant effects for the total score ($\underline{F}(3,6) = 17.48$, $p = .002$), and each of the three subscales: Teacher-Preferred Behavior ($\underline{F}(3,6) = 8.34$, $p = .01$), Peer-Preferred Behavior ($\underline{F}(3,6) = 7.28$, $p = .02$), and School Adjustment ($\underline{F}(3,6) = 5.93$, $\underline{p} = .03$).

Table 5

Mean Scores for Treated Children on Teacher Ratings of

Social Skills Across Time

	Pre-Trt	Post-Trt	Fup 1	Fup 2	
	$\underline{M}$	$\underline{M}$	$\underline{M}$	$\underline{M}$	$\underline{F}(3,6)$
	$(\underline{SD})$	$(\underline{SD})$	$(\underline{SD})$	$(\underline{SD})$	
Walker-McConnell					
Total	96.8	130.2	135.4	114.0	17.48**
	(25.8)	(32.5)	(36.0)	(25.5)	
Teach. Prefer.	34.1	47.2	47.2	41.9	8.34**
	(9.7)	(10.2)	(13.1)	(11.2)	
Peer Prefer.	37.4	51.4	55.8	47.0	7.28*
	(15.2)	(14.0)	(15.0)	(9.4)	
Sch. Adjust.	21.9	31.6	32.4	25.1	5.93*
	(7.5)	(9.4)	(10.4)	(6.6)	

$\underline{N}$ = 9
* $p < .05$ ** $p < .01$

The results of polynomial contrasts for this social
skills measure differed somewhat from those reported above
for the disruptive behavior variables. Both the first and
second degree contrasts were significant for the Walker-
McConnell total score, Teacher-Preferred Behavior subscale,
and Peer-Preferred subscale. Plotted mean scores, shown in
Figures 9 - 11, illustrate that treatment gains evident at

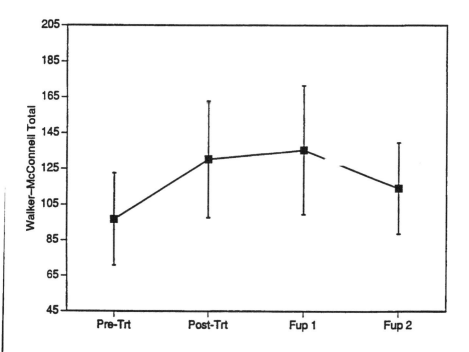

Figure 9. Mean Walker-McConnell social skills total scores
for treated children across four assessments with error
bars denoting 1 standard deviation.

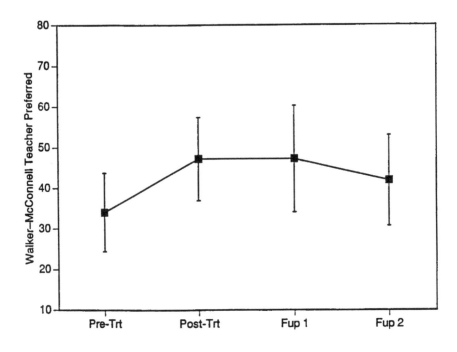

Figure 10. Mean Walker-McConnell social skills teacher preferred behavior subscale for treated children across four assessments, with error bars denoting 1 standard deviation.

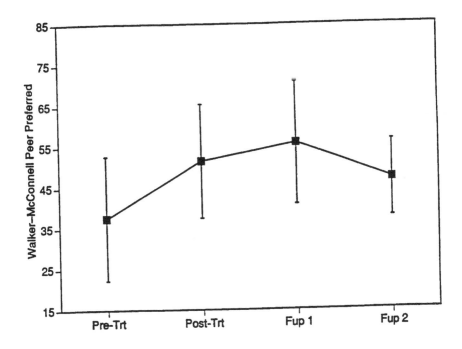

Figure 11. Mean Walker-McConnell social skills peer preferred behavior subscale for treated children across four assessments, with error bars denoting 1 standard deviation.

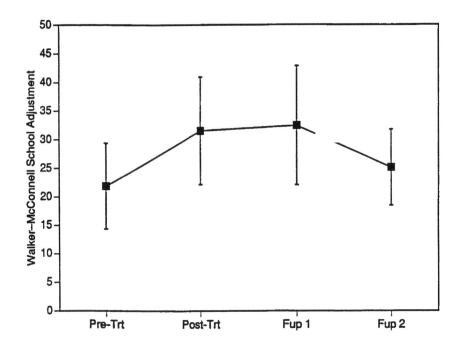

Figure 12. Mean Walker-McConnell social skills school
adjustment subscale for treated children across four
assessments, with error bars denoting 1 standard deviation.

posttreatment were maintained or improved at the 12-month followup, followed by a relatively mild decline at the 18-month followup. Scores at both followups remained within one standard deviation of posttreatment scores, and all scores at the 12-month followup were more than one standard deviation above pretreatment levels. At the 18-month followup, scores remained within one standard deviation of posttreatment outcome, but also fell within one standard deviation of the pretreatment level. For the School Adjustment subscale of the Walker-McConnell, only the second degree, or quadratic contrast, achieved significance. This quadratic pattern, illustrated in Figure 12, is consistent with the other Walker-McConnell results in showing improvement from posttreatment to 12-month followup. However, there is a steeper decline in scores from 12-month to 18-month followup than for the other social skills variables. Polynomial contrast results for the Walker-McConnell are shown in Table 6.

Parent Ratings

Mothers' ratings on the ECBI were available for a subset of children at both followup assessments. Mean ECBI scores across the four time intervals are shown in Table 7. Analysis of variance revealed significant effects for both the Intensity scale ($\underline{F}(3,5) = 6.55$, $p = .03$) and the Problem scale ($\underline{F}(3,4) = 11.81$ $p = .02$). Polynomial contrasts for the ECBI Intensity scale were significant for the first ($\underline{F}(1,7) = 14.67$, $p = .006$), second ($\underline{F}(1,7) = 16.72$, $p =$

.005), and third degree ($\underline{F}(1,7) = 10.20$, p = .015). As shown in Figure 13, ECBI intensity scores showed a sharp decline from pre- to posttreatment, followed by a gradual but significant increasing trend across the followup assessments. Polynomial contrasts for the Problem scale were significant for the first degree ($\underline{F}(1,6) = 17.14$, $\underline{p} = $ .006), and second degree ($\underline{F}(1,6) = 5.95$, $\underline{p} = .05$), and approached significance for the third degree contrast ($\underline{F}(1,6) = 5.06$, p = .06). The plotted problem score means, shown in Figure 14, show a steep pre- to posttreatment decline followed by a significant increase at first followup and a slight decline at second followup. Scores for the ECBI intensity and problem scores are above published clinical cutoffs at pretreatment and well within the normal range at the three other assessment intervals.

To evaluate the effect of outliers or of distinct subsets of subjects on the overall treatment group results, plots of individual subjects' scores across assessments were generated for each variable. No readily discernible patterns emerged from these data, which are presented in Appendix M. The number of children who maintained 30% gains over pretreatment scores was also calculated for each variable at the 12-month and 18-month followups, adopting the criteria used by McNeil et al. (1991) in the original school generalization study to define clinically significant improvement. The current findings, shown in Table 8, echo the results of the group ANOVAs, with percent compliance and the RCTRS Conduct Problem factor showing the strongest maintenance effects across followups. Teacher ratings showed greater decrements between the 12-month and 18-month followups in the number of children maintaining significant improvements than did behavioral observation variables.

Table 6

Polynomial Contrast Values for Mean Walker-McConnell Social Skills Ratings Across Time

| | Polynomial Contrast Values | | | | | |
| | 1st Degree | | 2nd Degree | | 3rd Degree | |
	$F_{(1,8)}$	p	$F_{(1,8)}$	p	$F_{(1,8)}$	p
Walker-McConnell						
Total	7.23	.028	27.14	.001	0.0	n.s.
Teacher-Prefer	10.23	.013	15.08	.005	0.23	n.s.
Peer-Prefer	5.24	.051	19.12	.002	0.04	n.s.
School Adjust.	1.77	n.s.	22.52	.002	0.0	n.s.

Note. $N = 9$

Treatment vs. Comparison Children

The original McNeil et al. (1991) school generalization study used multivariate analysis of variance to explore differences from pretreatment to posttreatmentamong treated children and matched untreated control subjects. Because

followup assessments included the same treated children at
both assessments but different comparison children for each
assessment, a standard multivariate analysis of variance
with two groups (treatment and control) and time as a
repeated factor was not applicable. Instead, difference
scores were created and analyzed for each of the dependent
variables.

Table 7

Mean Scores for Treated Children on the Eyberg Child
Behavior Inventory

		Pre-Trt	Post-Trt	Fup 1	Fup 2	
	N	M	M	M	M	F
		(SD)	(SD)	(SD)	(SD)	(df)
ECBI						
Intensity	8	169.9	101.9	114.8	119.1	6.55[*]
		(32.4)	(14.5)	(18.0)	(13.6)	(3,5)
Problem	7	21.1	4.8	10.3	7.1	11.81[*]
		(6.2)	(3.2)	(10.8)	(5.8)	(3,4)

[*] $p < .05$ [**] $p < .01$

Three difference scores were created per dependent
variable at each followup by subtracting the score of each
comparison child from that of the treated child (i.e.,
treated child's score minus "fewest behavior problems"

comparison subject's score, treated child's score minus "average behavior problems" comparison subject's score, and treated child's score minus "most behavior problems" comparison subject's score).

Table 8

Number of Children Maintaining 30% Improvement Over PreTreatment Baseline at Followup

	Followup 1	Followup 2
Behavioral Observations		
% Compliance	6	7
% Appropriate	4	4
% On Task	2	4
Conduct Ratings		
SESBI Intensity	5	3
SESBI Problem	8	5
RCTRS Hyp. Index	6	4
RCTRS Conduct Prob.	8	6
Social Skills Ratings		
Total	8	5
Teacher Preferred		3
Peer Preferred	5	
School Adjustment	6	5

Note. N = 10 at 12-month Followup; N = 11 at 18-month followup.

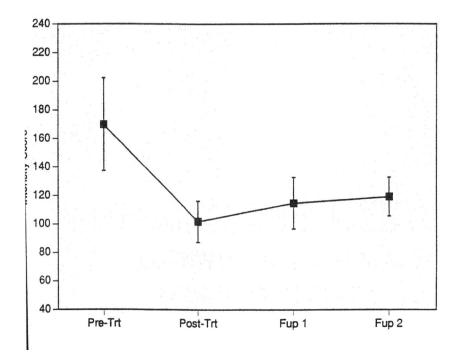

Figure 13. Mean ECBI Intensity Scores for treated children across four assessments, with error bars denoting 1 standard deviation ($\underline{N}$ = 8).

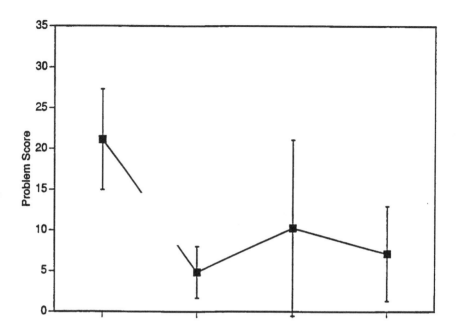

<u>Figure 14</u>. Mean ECBI Problem Scores for treated children
across four assessments, with error bars denoting 1 standard
deviation ($\underline{N}$ = 7).

The hypothesis that the treated group did not differ significantly from comparison children (i.e., the mean difference between comparison children and treated children was equal to zero) was tested for each dependent variable using Hotelling's T^2 separately for the 12-month and the 18-month followups. Next the magnitude of the difference across time between the treated group and comparison groups was examined using Hotelling's T^2 for dependent samples, a multivariate generalization of the paired t-test (Tabachnick & Fidell, 1989, p 447). This tested the hypothesis that the vector of treatment-to-comparison difference scores found at the 18-month followup would be identical to that of the 12-month followup results.

To control for multiple comparisons, Holm's sequentially rejective procedure was applied (Holm, 1979). Dependent variables were grouped into three sets: behavior observation variables, teacher behavior problem ratings, and social skills ratings. The multivariate hypothesis for each dependent variable required a significance level of .05 divided by the number of variables in the set (i.e., .05/3 = .017 for behavioral observations; .05/5 = .01 for teacher ratings; and .05/4 = .0125 for social skills ratings). To determine the protected alpha level for pairwise comparisons, pairwise test values were first sequenced from largest to smallest. The largest two test values required an alpha equal to the multivariate test alpha divided by two

12-Month Followup

Behavioral observations. Mean scores for the treated children and comparison children on the behavioral observation measures at each followup are shown in Table 9. Within the 12-month followup, only the appropriate behavior variable showed a significant difference across mean difference scores ($T^2 = 4.24$, p = .006). This finding was followed up with pairwise comparisons, of which the comparison between the treated child and "few problems" comparison child was sizable, but not statistically significant ($t = -2.02$, p = .07). Pairwise comparisons for the treated child versus the other two comparison groups did not approach significance for the appropriate behavior variable. Tests of the compliance variable ($T^2 = 1.05$, n.s.) and the on-task variable ($T^2 = 1.52$, n.s.) were not significant, perhaps due to the relatively restricted variation and large standard deviations across comparison groups. As Table 9 shows, the treatment group showed compliance mean scores slightly below the "behavior problem" comparison group, while their mean appropriate and on task scores were slightly above those of the "behavior problem" and "middle problems" comparison groups at the 12-month followup. In summary, the treated group did not differ significantly from the comparison children on observational

The data were noteworthy for a high degree of overlap between the "average problems" and "most problems" comparison groups.

Table 9

Mean Percentages on Observational Measures per Followup

	12- Month Followup		18-Month Followup	
	Mean	S.D.	Mean	S.D.
Compliance				
Treated	77.6	14.6	77.5	17.2
Low Problems	91.3	9.9	92.5	12.6
Avg. Problems	81.4	16.4	81.7	17.6
High Problems	79.6	19.4	71.4	23.7
Appropriate				
Treated	87.1	12.9	77.4	11.5
Low Problems	96.3	3.5	92.5	6.7
Avg. Problems	83.1	7.1	92.2	4.8
High Problems	85.0	9.6	84.5	12.2
On Task				
Treated	81.3	14.6	71.1	12.7
Low Problems	90.6	6.7	90.1	9.0
Avg. Problems	79.5	12.1	85.9	8.6
High Problems	79.4	11.8	79.4	10.6

Note. $\underline{N}$ = 10 at 12-month Followup; $\underline{N}$ = 11 at 18-month followup.

Teacher ratings. Table 10 shows mean scores for the treatment and comparison children on the SESBI and Conners for each followup assessment. Analyses of the 12-month data showed significant differences across the vector of treated-minus-comparison scores for both scales of the SESBI and all three of the Conners factors evaluated. Hotelling's T^2 values and significance levels are shown in Table 11. Pairwise comparisons revealed that the treatment-versus-"average" comparison was not significant for any variable, meaning that treated children did not differ significantly from this group. The contrasts between treated and "most problems" comparison children were sizable for the SESBI Intensity scale ($\underline{t}$ = - 3.04, p = .01), the Conners Hyperactivity Index ($\underline{t}$ = - 3.26, $\underline{p}$ = .01), and the Conners Conduct Problem factor ($\underline{t}$ = - 3.02, p = .01) (indicating that treated children showed fewer problems), but these comparisons were not significant at the alpha levels required to control for multiple comparisons ((.05/5)/2 = .005). Treatment-versus-"few problem" comparisons were significant for the SESBI Intensity scale ($\underline{t}$ = 3.87, $\underline{p}$ = .004), and the Conners Hyperactivity Index ($\underline{t}$ = 4.15, p = .002), indicating that treated children showed more problems than the "few problems" comparison group on these variables. Comparisons were also sizable for the SESBI Problem scale ($\underline{t}$ = 2.48, p = .04), and the Conners Conduct Problem factor ($\underline{t}$ = 3.40, $\underline{p}$ = .008), although these pairwise comparisons were

Table 10

Mean Scores on Teacher Ratings per Followup

	Followup 1		Followup 2	
	Mean	S.D.	Mean	S.D.
SESBI Intensity				
Treated	113.4	38.0	138.7	43.3
Low Problems	59.4	22.8	49.6	16.1
Avg. Problems	105.1	24.4	98.9	34.0
High Problems	142.9	20.2	142.4	45.4
SESBI Problem				
Treated	8.5	8.4	15.3	8.8
Low Problems	1.1	2.3	1.2	2.1
Avg. Problems	6.9	7.6	9.0	5.1
High Problems	14.3	5.7	18.4	7.5
Conners Hyperactivity Index				
Treated	1.41	.75	1.87	.82
Low Problems	.24	.32	.24	.20
Avg. Problems	1.06	.62	1.12	.64
High Problems	1.92	.53	1.86	.83
Conners Conduct Problem				
Treated	.97	.56	1.02	.68
Low Problems	.22	.24	.19	.20
Avg. Problems	.81	.62	.85	.75
High Problems	1.45	.50	1.65	1.04

Treated	1.27	.89	1.67	.72
Low Problems	.64	.55	.43	.56
Avg. Problems	1.16	.75	1.10	.81
High Problems	1.76	.62	1.38	.79

Note. N = 10 at 12-month followup; N = 11 at 18-month followup.

not significant at protected alpha levels. Taken together, these results indicate that at the 12-month followup, treated children fell within the range of "average" comparison children on all teacher rating measures of classroom behavior problems. Mean scores indicated lower levels of behavior problems than the "most behavior problems" comparison children on some variables, but these differences were not significant at protected levels. Scores on the SESBI Intensity scale and the Conners Hyperactivity Index did indicate significantly more problems than those of the "fewest behavior problems" comparison group.

Social skills ratings. Mean scores for the treated and comparison children at each followup on the total and subscale scores of the Walker McConnell are shown in Table 12. Higher scores represent greater social competence on scores on the Walker-McConnell total score (T^2 = 6.38, p = .002), and the Teacher-Preferred Behavior subscale (T^2 = 3.52, p = .01).

Table 11

Hotelling's T^2 Values for Teacher Rating Variables at 12-Month Followup

	Hotelling's T^2	p-value
SESBI Intensity	6.40	.002
SESBI Problem	5.84	.003
Conners Hyp. Index	14.61	.001
Conners Cond. Prob.	3.94	.008
Conners Inatt. Pass.	3.31	.013

Note. N = 10

Pairwise comparisons revealed that treated children scored significantly higher on social competence than the "most problems" comparison group on both the total score (t = 4.79, p = .002), and the Teacher Preferred Behavior subscale (t = 3.14, p = .01). As Table 12 shows, treated children showed mean scores that were very similar to the "average problems" comparison group and uniformly higher (i.e., more competent) than the "most problems" comparison

Table 12

Mean Scores on Walker McConnell per Followup

	12-Month Followup		18-Month Followup	
	Mean	S.D.	Mean	S.D.
Total Score				
Treated	137.9	34.8	115.0	43.3
Few Problems	156.5	37.5	176.9	16.1
Avg. Problems	141.8	30.0	129.7	34.0
Most Problems	107.2	23.1	114.5	45.4
Teacher Preferred				
Treated	48.4	12.9	42.6	11.4
Few Problems	60.5	12.3	64.7	8.6
Avg. Problems	51.9	10.3	46.3	9.1
Most Problems	39.2	6.1	39.1	11.9
Peer Preferred				
Treated	56.6	14.4	46.6	8.6
Few Problems	55.9	17.6	67.7	11.4
Avg. Problems	57.0	14.4	53.2	14.6
Most Problems	42.8	13.0	49.7	10.7
School Adjustment				
Treated	32.9	9.9	25.7	6.1
Few Problems	40.1	9.8	44.5	6.4
Avg. Problems	32.9	9.8	30.0	8.7
Most Problems	25.2	7.0	26.6	7.1

Note. N = 10 at 12-month Followup; N = 11 at 18-month followup.

group for all subscales of the Walker-McConnell at the 12-month followup. Hotelling's T^2 values were sizable for the Peer Preferred Behavior subscale ($\underline{T}^2$ = 2.81, $\underline{p}$ = .02) and the School Adjustment subscale ($\underline{T}^2$ = 2.82, $\underline{p}$ = .02), but these did not reach significance at the protected alpha level (i.e., .05/4 = .0125).

18-Month Followup

Behavioral observations. Mean scores for the 18-month followup behavioral observation measures are shown in Table 9 for the treated and comparison children. Only the on-task measure ($\underline{T}^2$ = 3.04, p = .008) showed significant variation within the vector of treatment-versus-comparison difference scores. Pairwise comparisons indicated that treated children showed lower percentages of on-task behavior than the "few problems" comparison group ($\underline{t}$ = - 4.34, $\underline{p}$ = .002), and the "average" comparison group ($\underline{t}$ = - 5.29, p = .0004) at the 18-month followup. The treatment group's on task mean scores were also lower than those of the "behavior problem" comparison group, although this comparison ($\underline{t}$ = -2.57, p = .03) was not significant at the protected alpha level (i.e., (.05/3)/2 = .008). The treatment group's mean compliance score fell solidly within the middle range of the comparison groups (see Table 9) at the 18-month followup, and the Hotelling's T^2 test ($\underline{T}^2$ = .73, n.s.) did not approach significance. On the appropriate variable, the treatment group had the lowest mean percentage of appropriate behavior (see Table G), but the overall effect

(T^2 = 1.73, p = .04) was not significant at the protected alpha level (i.e., .05/3 = .017). Taken together, these results indicate that the treated children fell somewhere within the observed range of classroom behaviors at the 18-month followup in terms of compliance and percentage of appropriate behavior, while their percentage of on-task behavior fell near or below the range of the "behavior problems" comparison group.

Table 13

Hotelling's T^2 Values for Teacher Rating Variables at 18-Month Followup

	Hotelling's T^2	p-value
SESBI Intensity	5.30	.002
SESBI Problem	7.52	.001
Conners Hyp. Index	5.78	.001
Conners Cond. Prob.	2.74	.011
Conners Inatt. Pass.	3.17	.007

N = 11

Teacher ratings. Table 10 shows mean scores at the 18-month followup for the treated and comparison children on the SESBI and Conners rating scales. Mean scores show that treatment group scores were similar to those of the "most problems" comparison group on every measure. Hotelling's T^2

tests indicated significant effects for each variable, and these values are shown in Table 13.

Pairwise comparisons indicated that the treatment group showed significantly more problems than the "few problems" comparison group on all measures evaluated: the SESBI Intensity scale (t = 6.67, p = .0001), the SESBI Problem scale (t = 5.44, p = .0003), the Conners Hyperactivity Index (t = 7.15, p = .0001), the Conners Conduct Problem factor (t = 4.22, p = .002), and the Conners Inattentive-Passive factor (t = 5.39, p = .0003). Pairwise comparisons also separated the treatment group from the "average" comparison group on the SESBI intensity score (t = 3.62, p = .005). Pairwise comparisons contrasting the treatment and "average" groups were sizable, but did not reach protected significance levels (i.e., (.05/5)/2 = .005) for the SESBI problem score (t = 2.57, p = .03), the Conners Hyperactivity Index (t = 3.24, p = .009), and the Conners Inattentive-Passive factor (t = 2.24, p = .05). Only for the Conners Conduct Problem factor did the treatment group mean score fall nearer to the "average problems" comparison group than to the "most problems" comparison group at the 18-month followup. For this variable the pairwise comparison contrasting the treatment group to the behavior problem comparison group was sizeable (t = - 2.76, p = .02), although not significant at the protected alpha level.

Social skills ratings. Results on the Walker-McConnell social skills ratings at second followup (shown in

Table 12) closely resemble the other teacher rating measures reported above. Hotelling's T^2 values were significant for the total score and each of the three subscales, and post hoc pairwise comparisons indicated that the treatment group showed lower levels of social competence than the "few problems" comparison group on each variable. No other pairwise comparisons approached significance. Table 14 displays the values of the overall test and significant pairwise comparison values for the Walker-McConnell. It appears that the treatment group children fall within the range of the "average" and "most problems" comparison groups at the 18-month followup in terms of social skills, and clearly below the social skills level of children selected as presenting few classroom behavior problems.

Table 14

Hotelling's T^2 Values for Social Skills Ratings at 18-Month Followup

	T^2	p	t^*	p
Walker McConnell				
Total	5.74	.001	− 7.44	.0001
Teacher-Preferred	4.26	.003	− 6.08	.0001
Peer-Preferred	3.77	.004	− 5.52	.0003
School Adjustment	11.81	.0001	−10.65	.0001

Note. N = 11
* t-test for treatment group versus "few problems" comparison group

12-Month and 18-Month Followups Compared

Behavioral observations. Comparison of consistency of
results across the two followup assessments revealed that
the profile of mean difference scores within the 12-month
followup varied significantly from that of the 18-month
followup for the behavioral observation measures of
appropriate behavior and on-task behavior. The Hotelling's
T^2 value of .05, n.s., for the compliance variable indicated
that there was no significant change in the relative
positioning of the treated and comparison children between
the two followup assessments on that variable. As Table 9
shows, treated children maintained virtually the same level
of compliance at each followup assessment.

For the appropriate behavior variable, the Hotelling's
T^2 of 5.49, p = .008, indicated a significant change in the
magnitude of difference scores across followups. Pairwise
comparisons between the treatment group and "most problems"
comparison children (t = -3.30, p = .01) and between the
treatment group and "average" comparison children (t =
-3.01, p = .02) were sizable, but did not reach significance
levels required to control for multiple comparisons. The
Hotelling's T^2 of 5.51, p = .008, was significant for the
on-task variable, demonstrating a significant change in the
treated children's position relative to comparison children
across followup assessments. Pairwise comparisons were
again sizable for the treated children compared with the
"most problems" comparison group (t = -4.93, p = .001) and

the treated children compared with the "average problems"
comparison group (t = -2.04, p = .08), although only the
treated child versus behavior problem comparison child
contrast was significant (again controlling for multiple
comparisons). These results indicate that the treatment
child moved from out of the range of the "most problems"
comparison children at the 12-month followup to within their
range at the 18-month followup. Table 9 demonstrates the
shift in the treated child's relative position on the
appropriate and on-task variables. At the 12-month
followup, the treated child showed slightly higher levels of
appropriate and on-task behavior than the "average" and
"most problems" comparison children. Treated children
showed a decline in appropriate behavior and on-task
behavior at the 18-month followup, and these scores fell
below the appropriate and on task scores of the "average"
and "most problems" comparison children. Table 9 also
illustrates the fairly consistent scores of the comparison
subjects across followups despite the fact that a different
set of comparison children was used for each assessment.

Teacher ratings. Tests of the multivariate hypothesis
of equality of difference score vectors across the two
followups for teacher ratings yielded mixed results. The
Hotelling's T^2 for the SESBI intensity score (T^2 = 4.25, p =
.01) showed significant downward shifts in the treated
children relative to comparison children. Pairwise
comparisons, corrected for multiple comparisons, showed

sizable differences on the SESBI intensity score in the treated versus "few problems" comparison child difference score ($\underline{t}$ = 5.02, p = .001) and the treated versus "average" comparison child difference score ($\underline{t}$ = 2.73, p = .02), although only the former was significant at the protected $\underline{p}$-value. Hotelling's T^2 for the Conners Hyperactivity Index ($\underline{T}^2$ = 2.70, p = .04), although sizable, did not reach significance at the protected alpha level (i.e., .05/5 = .01). Hotelling's T^2 results were not significant for the SESBI problem score, the Conners Conduct Problem factor, or the Conners Inattentive-Passive factor, indicating that there were no significant shifts in the difference score profiles for these variables. Review of Table 10 reveals that, similar to the behavioral observation findings, treated children exhibited more behavior problems at the 18-month followup while scores for the two sets of comparison children remained relatively consistent across followups. At the 12-month followup, the scores of treated children generally fell between those of the "average" comparison children and the "most problems" comparison children. At the 18-month followup, their scores appear most similar to those of the behavior problem comparison children, with the largest shift occurring in the SESBI intensity score.

Social skills ratings. Evaluation of the stability of findings across the two followup assessments on the Walker McConnell social skills measure did not reveal changes that were significant at protected alpha levels. Although fairly large downward shifts were reflected in Hotelling's T^2 scores for the test of the total score (T^2 = 1.90, p = .08), the Peer Preferred behavior subscale (T^2 = 3.22, p = .03), and the School Adjustment subscale (T^2 = 3.09, p = .03), these did not reach significance at the protected alpha level (i.e., .05/4 = .01).

Comparison of Two vs. Three Days of Classroom Observation

The design of the present study included three days of observation in the classroom. The original McNeil et al. (1991) school generalization study included only two days of classroom observation. The observation period was extended for the present study in part because of the presence of three rather than two comparison subjects like in the McNeil et al. design. Extending observation periods within a two-day period was not feasible because the behavioral coding system requires relatively structured activities which occur for a short portion of the day in most preschool and early elementary classrooms.

It was hoped that adding a third day of observations would strengthen the validity of the data and provide a clearer picture of the treated and comparison children. However, each additional day of classroom observation incurs substantial costs in terms of scheduling, transportation, and coders' time. It was therefore desirable to evaluate the data in terms of the relative value of the third day of observation. The sample size of the present study was felt to be too small to permit confident interpretation of statistical tests such as regression analysis of incremental value of days of observation. Rather, a more pragmatic approach was chosen of re-running the treatment-versus-comparison group statistics using two days of observation rather than three.

Results of the two-day analyses yielded exactly the same findings for Followup 1 and for Followup 2. Table 15 presents the comparative results. However, Table 15 also shows that when the 12-month and 18-month findings were compared, the two-day results did not completely replicate the three-day observation results. Three days of observation indicated a significant shift in the appropriate behavior variable across followups, although none of the pairwise comparisons were interpretable at protected alpha levels. Two days of observations did not indicate a significant shift for the appropriate behavior variable. The on task variable showed more discrepant results, with three-day data indicating a significant shift across followups. Pairwise comparisons with the three-day data confirmed that treatment children shifted significantly in the direction of the "most problems" comparison group from first to second followup. Two-day observations failed to pick up any significant trend in the on-task behavior variable across followups. Table 16 shows the results of pairwise comparisons for the 12-month versus 18-month contrast based on two days and three days of observation for the appropriate and on task variables. Pairwise comparisons were not appropriate for the compliance variable because the result of the multivariate test was not significant.

Table 15

Comparison of 2 Days versus 3 Days of Classroom Observations for Multivariate Tests

| | Two Days | | Three Days | |
	T^2	p	T^2	p
12-Month Followup				
Compliance	.64	n.s.	1.05	n.s.
Appropriate	4.54	.005	4.23	.006
On Task	1.45	n.s.	1.52	n.s.
18-Month Followup				
Compliance	.78	n.s.	.73	n.s.
Appropriate	2.03	.02	1.73	.04
On Task	5.92	.001	3.04	.008
12-Month vs. 18-Month Followups				
Compliance	.05	n.s.	.05	n.s.
Appropriate	2.70	.04	5.49	.007
On Task	1.06	n.s.	5.51	.008

Table 16

Pairwise Comparisons Based on 2 Days and 3 Days of

Classroom Observations for 12-Month vs. 18-Month Followups

	Treated vs Few		Treated vs Average		Treated vs Most	
	t	p	t	p	t	p
Appropriate						
2 days	.69	n.s.	2.45	.04	1.59	n.s.
3 days	.88	n.s.	3.01	.02	3.30	.01
On Task						
2 days	1.36	n.s.	1.87	n.s.	2.71	.03
3 days	1.41	n.s.	2.04	n.s.	4.93	.001[*]

[*] significant at protected level

CHAPTER 4
DISCUSSION

The results of this study demonstrated maintenance of school generalization of behavioral improvements up to 12 months following completion of PCIT treatment. Group means for compliance and conduct problem behavior at the 12-month followup were very similar to posttreatment scores on observational and rating scale measures. Although prior to treatment, the treatment group showed more behavior problems than even "deviant" control children on most measures (McNeil et al., 1991), they were indistinguishable from comparison children at the 12-month followup. In fact, at the 12-month followup the group mean for treated children was very similar to the group mean for the "average behavior" comparison group on most measures, including percent appropriate, both scales of the SESBI, and the RCTRS Conduct Problem factor.

The treatment group's mean compliance rate of 77.6% was slightly lower than group means for the "average behavior" comparison group (81.4%) and the "most behavior problems" comparison group (79.6%) at the 12-month followup, but this difference was not statistically significant and likely not clinically significant. As predicted by the PCIT model, treated children appear to have been "overtrained" in compliance by the end of treatment, with higher mean

101

compliance rates (i.e., 87%) than even the nondeviant control group (i.e., 80%) (McNeil et al., 1991). One-year posttreatment, the treatment group appeared to have settled into compliance rates that are more typical for normal school children, but still far higher than the pretreatment group mean compliance rate of 54%.

At the 18-month followup, treated children maintained significant improvement over pretreatment scores on observed compliance (i.e., 76%), but scores on other observational measures and teacher ratings showed a pronounced shift in the direction of pretreatment levels.
The treatment group's compliance percentage also compared favorably with comparison groups, falling nearest to the "average" group's mean compliance score. However, the treatment group appeared most similar to the "most problems" comparison group on all other observational and teacher rating measures at the 18-month followup. Mean scores for the treatment group indicated more problems than the "most problems" comparison group on observational measures of appropriate and on task behavior and on the RCTRS Hyperactivity Index, although these differences were not statistically significant. Scores for children in the treated group indicated significantly more problems than those of the "few problems" comparison group on a number of measures at the 18-month followup.

Treatment effects measured at the end of therapy were stronger for measures of compliance and oppositionality than for measures of attention and activity, and these differential effects were maintained at followup. Percent compliance, the RCTRS Conduct Problem factor, and the SESBI Problem scale showed the strongest maintenance at both the 12-month and the 18-month followups. Only three variables reverted to pretreatment mean levels at followup, and these were the attention-related measures: percent on task, RCTRS Hyperactivity Index, and RCTRS Inattentive-Passive factor.

A look at individual children corroborates this impression of stronger effects for compliance and conduct problem measures. Clinically significant improvements of 30% or more over pretreatment baseline were maintained on the compliance variable for 6 of 10 children at the 12-month followup and for 7 of 11 at the 18-month assessment. Similar results were found for the RCTRS Conduct Problem factor (8 of 10 at first followup and 6 of 11 at second followup) and the SESBI Problem scale (8 of 10 at first followup and 5 of 11 at second followup). In contrast, only 2 of 10 children maintained improvements on the on task measure at the 12-month followup and 4 of 11 at the 18-month followup. For the RCTRS Hyperactivity Index, 6 of 10 children maintained improvement 12 months posttreatment and 4 of 10 at the 18-month followup.

To summarize, the results of the 12-month followup confirmed the study's primary hypotheses by demonstrating maintenance of school generalization, with stronger effects for measures of compliance and conduct than for measures of attention. The results of the 18-month followup were unexpected, and lend credence to the warning that "there is no reason to assume a linear trend following treatment, and it is important that repeated measures are taken . . ." (Mash and Terdal, 1977, p. 1295).

It was hypothesized that social competence, which did not show significant improvements following treatment relative to controls, would continue to improve as a second order effect of treated children's increased compliance and decreased conduct problems. Indeed, the treatment group did show significant increases on the Walker McConnell social skills measures between posttreatment and the 12-month followup. It is difficult to rule out the possibility that maturation accounted for increases in social competence since the original control subjects were not re-evaluated. However, treated children showed higher ratings of social competence on all scales of the Walker McConnell than the "behavior problem" comparison group, and these differences were statistically significant for the Total score and the Teacher Preferred Behavior subscale. Mean scores in the treatment group were remarkably similar to the mean scores of the "average" comparison group at the 12-month followup. Some behavioral deterioration was noted between the followups such that, at the 18-month followup, the treatment group's mean scores were very similar to those of the "behavior problem" comparison group.

This initial evidence of continuing improvement on the Walker-McConnell during the year following the end of PCIT treatment is noteworthy because previous PMT studies have not found longterm improvements in social competence. It has been noted that "improving the social behavior of rejected boys is easier than improving their reputations or increasing peer acceptance" (Bierman, Miller, & Stabb, 1987, p. 199). That quote came in the context of a social skills training program for first-through-third-grade boys that demonstrated reductions in negative behavior but no improvements in teacher and peer aggression ratings at a one-year followup. The improvement of teacher ratings to within normal limits on the Peer Preferred Behavior subscale is particularly encouraging since it has been shown to be highly predictive of peer-nominated sociometric status (Walker & McConnell, 1987). Future research directly measuring sociometric status in children undergoing PCIT treatment would be enlightening both to determine whether these children are actually rejected by peers prior to treatment as would be predicted based on teacher ratings and behavioral observations, and to track their progress in the year following completion of treatment.

Previous research provides few answers to the question of why treatment effects would transfer into a new classroom at the 12-month followup, but falter in the transition into yet another new classroom at the 18-month followup. The few studies examining school generalization of PMT effects have

typically reported only a single followup that occurred a
year or less after the end of treatment (e.g., Sayger &
Horne, 1987; Strayhorn & Weidman, 1991; Webster-Stratton &
Hammond, 1990; Horn et al., 1990).

One well-controlled study that did assess followup on
more than one occasion involved a treatment program that
extended over two years and contained a PMT program as well
as social skills and other training components administered
directly to the children (Tremblay et al., 1991). Mothers'
ratings indicated an _increase_ in behavior problems at the
end of treatment, which calls into question the success of
the treatment and whether generalization to the classroom
should be expected. No improvements were noted on teacher
ratings at either the 1-year or the 2-year followup.

In the present study, information on children's and
parents' maintenance of treatment effects in the home would
aide in interpreting changes in children's school behavior
across the followup intervals. It can be hypothesized that
better school behavior at followup would be associated with
better maintenance of treatment gains in the home setting,
but that question was beyond the scope of the present study.
Clinic and home assessments of the treated children have
been collected in a separate PCIT outcome study, the results
of which are not yet available (Newcomb, 1993).

The sole parent report measure available in the present
study was the ECBI, and even this was not available for
several children. Although such a limited sample size

precluded any analysis beyond descriptive statistics, the results were not supportive of the notion of generalized behavioral decrements at the 18-month followup. On the contrary, ECBI scores remained solidly within the normal range at both the 12-month and 18-month followups. Although a nonsignificant increase in reported behavior problems occurred between posttreatment and the first followup, at the 18-month followup parents reported stable to slightly improved behavior relative to the 12-month followup. These findings are of course tentative, and ECBI ratings have consistently shown low correlations with teacher ratings on the SESBI (Funderburk & Eyberg, 1989; McNeil et al., 1991). However, McNeil and colleagues (1991) did find agreement between parents and teachers about the direction of change in children's behavior as measured by the ECBI and SESBI. It would appear from the current results that these parents report stable or improving behavior between 12 and 18 months following treatment, while the teachers report increasing behavior problems across the same interval.

It is tempting to account for the decline in scores at the 18-month followup as an artifact of having different teachers as informants at the two followups. However, teacher ratings of comparison children remained remarkably stable across assessments. Blind behavioral observations were also stable across assessments for comparison children, while the treatment group showed decrements in appropriate and on task behavior. This provides more evidence that bias in teachers' reporting could not account for the findings.

The accuracy of the mothers' ECBI scores was also examined since there was a possibility that the seven complete ECBIs available were not representative of the total sample. Personal communication with the principal investigator of the ongoing PCIT home and clinic followup revealed that ECBI scores were collected for 10 of the 12 school subjects 24 months following the end of treatment (K. Newcomb, personal communication, June 1, 1993). These scores (ECBI Intensity: 118; ECBI Problem: 6) were very similar to ECBI scores available in the current study (ECBI Intensity: 119; EGBI Problem: 7) at the 18-month assessment. Additional preliminary results available from K. Newcomb indicated that 3 of 10 children from this study met DSM-III-R diagnostic criteria at clinic assessments conducted one year and two years post treatment (K. Newcomb, personal communication, June 1, 1993). All subjects carried one or more disruptive behavior diagnoses prior to treatment, so it is encouraging that 7 of the 10 children followed in the clinic did not display serious enough behavior problems 24 months following treatment to qualify for a diagnosis.

In light of these findings, one should recall that despite 18-month followup behavioral decrements into the range of the "behavior problem" comparison group, even that comparison group represents normal variation in a nonreferred sample. In other words, 18 months following completion of treatment, treated children appeared similar to children at the high end of the normal range of classroom behavior problems. With regard to the "behavior problem" comparison group, teachers described 6 or 10 subjects as in need of treatment for behavior problems at the 12-month followup and 7 of 11 at the 18-month followup. Only 3 and 4 of the treated children were judged as needing treatment at the respective followups. Oddly, one child in the "average" comparison group (selected based on the teachers' ratings of average classroom behavior problems) for the 12-month followup and one "average" comparison child from the 18-month followup were judged by teachers as needing treatment for behavior problems. One of these ratings occurred in a regular third grade with an "average" child who had been referred for special educational services; the other occurred in a preschool classroom in which observers noted that the teacher appeared to have difficulty managing the class as a whole.

A strong association has been noted between ADHD and learning disabilities, leading Cantwell and Baker (1991, p. 90) to note that typically "these children are destined for school failure, learning problems, and/or learning disabilities." Eleven of the 12 children in the current treatment sample met diagnostic criteria for ADHD prior to treatment, with 10 of those also meeting criteria for ODD. Consistent with previous research, utilization of special educational services was high for the treatment group. By the 18-month followup 54% (6 of 11) were receiving special services. Learning problems were reported as the major reason for special educational services for 5 of the 6 children, while behavior problems (in addition to learning problems) were the primary concern for 1 child. These findings are particularly striking given the young age of the sample, which ranged from preschool to third grade at the time of the second followup. It is possible that the percentage of children receiving special educational services will increase as the youngest members of the group move into elementary school. Between one and three children (9% to 27%) from each comparison group were receiving special educational services except for the "behavior problem" comparison group at the 18-month followup, when 45% (5 of 11) were receiving special services.

These findings strengthen the impression that, while PCIT effectively increases compliance and reduces disruptive behaviors in the classroom for many children, it has little longterm effect on the academic and attentional problems associated with ADHD. However, it would be premature to conclude that PCIT should not be recommended for young ADHD children with school behavior problems. Campbell has concluded from her extensive work with disruptive preschoolers that younger hyperactive children tend to be more negative and noncompliant than older children with "pure" ADHD (Campbell, 1985). Although it would be desirable for research purposes to differentiate youngsters

with ADHD from those with ODD for separate treatment outcome
analyses, that may not be feasible for the preschool age
range.

Several attempts have been made to enhance PMT
treatment effects with ADHD children. Supplementing PMT and
cognitive-behavioral social skills training with three
scheduled therapist-teacher consultations during the course
of therapy did not improve school generalization in an
elementary school ADHD sample (Horn, Ialongo, Greenberg,
Packard, Smith-Winberry, 1990). More promising results for
ADHD symptoms were reported in a treatment program that
augmented PMT with positive relationship training and
training in the use of verbally encoded exchanges (e.g.,
stories, conversation, dramatic play) (Strayhorn & Weidman,
1991). Improved teacher ratings of ADHD symptoms were found
one year posttreatment in a sample of socioeconomically
disadvantaged preschoolers. However, this study involved
recruited children who did not all meet DSM-III-R diagnostic
criteria for ADHD, and the PMT portion of the treatment
reduced parent report of ADHD symptoms, but failed to
improve parent ratings of behavior problems or teacher
ratings of behavior and ADHD symptoms immediately after
treatment (Strayhorn & Weidman, 1989). Children who showed
the most improvement in the classroom at the one-year
followup tended to be the ones whose parents had shown
greatest improvement on behavioral observations of parent-
child interaction (Strayhorn & Weidman, 1991).

These results suggest that adding the promising verbal mediation elements of this treatment program to the proven effectiveness of PCIT for noncompliance and oppositionality might enhance the utility of PCIT for children with ADHD. Theorizing about elements of PCIT that may account for the demonstrated school generalization in the area of compliance and oppositionality, McNeil and colleagues noted several factors that differ from most PMT programs (McNeil et al., 1991). These include the focus on compliance as opposed to individual target behaviors, the emphasis on relationship enhancement which may reduce children's anger or self-esteem problems, and the structuring of the home environment in terms of consistent social rewards and behavioral consequences which may increase congruence between the classroom and home environments.

There are no clear standards as to what comprises successful longterm maintenance of treatment effects following PMT. Despite many demonstrations of treatment effects, most longterm research with disruptive behavior disorders documents continuing problems. For example, in a well-controlled study evaluating PMT as an adjunct to stimulant medication treatment, nine-month followup showed behavioral deterioration once medication was withdrawn, as well as minimal additive benefit from the combination treatment versus medication alone (Ialongo et al., 1993). On the other hand, a subset of 25% of the children who received the combined treatment did maintain treatment gains at the nine-month followup even when medication was withdrawn (Ialongo et al., 1993). These researchers and others have noted that a cost effective short-term treatment that yields longterm improvement in even a subset of cases may be a reasonable approach to take before proceeding with more extensive (and equally uncertain) interventions (Ialongo et al., 1993; Webster-Stratton et al., 1988).

Another relatively undefined issue regarding longterm treatment maintenance is which behaviors must be affected to denote success. PMT outcome studies routinely evaluate variables ranging from maternal depression to child's self-esteem to rates of targeted behaviors such as praise or compliance. Similarly, school maintenance has been assessed in terms of compliance and behavioral variables, in terms of social acceptance, referrals for special services, or even academic success. With PMT treatment programs typically limited to 8 to 12 weeks duration, the question has been posed: ". . . are our expectations about the long-term effects of our interventions reasonable? Are we not asking too much when we expect that a treatment will continue to have desired effects long after its discontinuation?" (Kendall & Koehler, 1985, p. 110).

In considering a chronic illness model for the conceptualization of disruptive behavior disorders, Kazdin noted that "the conventional model of treatment for conduct disorder is to administer a particular intervention over a period of time (e.g., weeks or months), to terminate the treatment, and to hope for or marvel at the permanent changes" (Kazdin, 1987, p. 199). He suggests that it may be useful to consider conduct disorder a chronic condition which will require ongoing treatment and evaluation in somewhat the sense that insulin treatment for diabetes must be maintained, monitored, and adjusted throughout the lifespan of the diabetic (Kazdin, 1987). Taking this long view, PCIT would appear to be an ideal "first stage" treatment given its appropriateness to young children, the breadth of its coverage, and its generalization to at least some facets of school adjustment and social competency.

One of the primary limitations of the current study is the small sample size, which constrains the power of statistical analyses and limits the confidence with which findings can be generalized. Evaluating a relatively large number of dependent variables (with appropriate multiple-comparison controls) in such a small sample required large effects to achieve significance. The high rate of participation of available subjects (92% for 12-month followup and 100% for 18-month followup) maximized the current sample's potential, but replication in future studies with larger samples will be important. Given that this sample comprised the first demonstrated successful school generalization of PCIT, the importance of monitoring the longterm maintenance of effects in these children was felt to outweigh the admittedly heavy methodological drawbacks. At at minimum, the current study would certainly seem to indicate the need for future researchers interested in school maintenance to extend followup past one year rather than assuming that effects will endure indefinitely at full strength.

The sample size of the present study did not permit statistical analysis of the effects of stimulant medication on longterm school maintenance. Two children who participated in both followup assessments, one who participated in only the 12-month followup, and one who participated only in the 18-month followup had been placed on stimulant medication following the end of treatment. One child was on stimulant medication throughout treatment and both followups. Inspection of plots overlaying each treated child's scores on individual variables did not reveal any consistent pattern for children receiving medication that would suggest differential outcome relative to nonmedicated children (see Appendix M). Interestingly, the medicated subjects followed the same pattern of behavioral deterioration between the 12-month and 18-month followups. Ongoing medication could have been expected to support more stable improvements. The plots suggest that teacher ratings, particularly the SESBI Intensity Score and the RCTRS Hyperactivity Index and Inattentive-Passive factor, showed greater improvements for the children receiving medication than did observational measures.

Like medication status at followup, teachers' knowledge of the children's treatment status was an uncontrolled variable in this applied research setting. Although the researcher did not inform them of children's treatment status, a surprising number of teachers (64% at 12-month followup and 73% at 18-month followup) were able to identify students who had received PCIT treatment. This information typically came from parent conferences and discussions with previous teachers. It is unclear whether such low rates of blind teacher ratings could be expected in any early elementary school sample or whether the current group may have maintained an unusually "high profile" due to the relatively severe nature of their pretreatment problems and their participation in the original school generalization research. In either case, the consistency found between teacher ratings and behavioral observations by blind observers allays concern about possible teacher bias.

Although including classroom behavioral observations increases the validity of findings over reliance on teacher ratings alone, live coding in the preschool and elementary classroom does present a challenge in terms of reliable coding. Most PMT investigations that include behavioral observation data have reported reliability in terms of percent agreement (McNeil et al., 1991; Strain et al., 1982; Webster-Stratton & Hammond, 1990; Webster-Stratton et al., 1989; Wells & Egan, 1988). This method of reliability calculation has been criticized as potentially inflating agreement scores by failing to control for chance agreements. For example, in the present study a high rate of chance agreement could be expected for the category of global appropriate because there are only two possible responses: appropriate or inappropriate.

Percent agreement figures reported in the studies referenced above ranged from 80% to 92% for overall agreement and from 74% to 97% for individual behavior categories such as child compliance. These agreement percentages are comparable to percent agreements in the present study which ranged from .83 for compliance to .89 for appropriate behavior. One would expect higher interrater reliability from coding of videotaped segments than from live coding, because the videotaped observations can be viewed again and again. In a pilot project preceding the original school generalization study we attempted videotaping preschool classroom observations. This did not prove feasible due to frequent location shifts in preschool (and early elementary) classes from one "activity" center to another. The videotape equipment in the classroom also appeared to be much more distracting to the young children than the presence of live coders. One PMT outcome study that did report Kappa for live coding of home behavioral observations collapsed categories to yield high Kappa values of .79 for overall child behaviors and .83 for overall parent behaviors (Dadds & McHugh, 1992). Kappa values for specific categories of behavior were not included in that report.

Kappa statistics for the three behavior observation variables in the current study were as follows: .56 for global ratings of appropriate behavior; .59 for ratings of appropriate behavior by specific categories; .65 for compliance, and .66 for on task behavior. It has been suggested that Kappas of .60 - .75 represent "good" agreement and Kappas of .40 to .60 signify "fair" agreement (Fleiss, 1981). Other researchers suggest stricter standards of above .70 for acceptable reliability (Bakeman & Gottman, 1986). The Kappa statistics reported in the present study are felt to represent adequate interrater reliability given the use of live coding, the high chance rate of agreement inherent in the chosen coding system, and the uniformity of reliability results across individual coders and individual children (see Table 1). It is hoped that clearer guidelines for what constitutes acceptable interrater agreement will emerge.

Another relatively undefined issue in school generalization research is the acceptable selection and use of control groups. As mentioned previously, the majority of school outcome studies have relied on teacher rating measures of the treated child with no use of controls. Treatment outcome studies often employ wait-list controls, which results in a control group that is lost to followup assessment since most subjects on the waiting list eventually receive treatment. Other studies have employed anonymous control subjects that cannot be identified for followup. This was the case for the school generalization study which prompted the current research. Pilot work prior to the original study revealed great difficulty obtaining consent from families of the more deviant children in the classroom, so that blind observations were chosen as a more effective method of obtaining control data. Even if control children could be identified at followup, they would in many cases be in different classrooms from the treated child. These control subjects would then continue to control for demographic variables and maturational effects but would no longer be appropriate controls in terms of classroom environment effects.

This raises the crucial issue of the purpose of the selected control group. The McNeil et al. (1991) study employed "deviant" classroom controls (identified by school personnel as having behavior problems) to serve the function of an untreated control group. The same study also employed nondeviant classroom controls (identified by school personnel as showing "average" behavior) whose scores were used to define classroom "normal limits" in the evaluation of the clinical significance of treatment effects (McNeil et al., 1991). Followup school studies generally employ comparison children from the current classroom to control for situational variables and to define normal limits (Walker and Hops, 1976). Strain and colleagues (1982) randomly selected four gender- and age-matched classmates for normative comparisons. Campbell & Ewing (1990) recruited comparison children from the current classrooms of study children to compensate for control subject attrition in a longitudinal study.

The present study sought to determine where treated children fell on the continuum of behaviors in their present classroom; comparison subjects were chosen to approximate the full behavioral range of each class. Every effort was made to ensure that the teacher was not aware of which comparison children were selected until after classroom observations were complete. It was felt that true random selection of comparison subjects would have required more comparison children to represent confidently the classroom behavioral spectrum.

To further assure the representativeness of the data, behavioral observations were collected on three days whenever possible, rather than on two occasions as in the McNeil et al. study (1991). The utility of including a third day was evaluated by re-analyzing the data based on the first two days of observation. The re-analysis did not result in any different outcome for the 12-month or 18-month followup. However, some evidence of incremental power from the third day of observation was shown in the re-analysis of the test of the hypothesis that 12-month outcomes were equal to 18-month outcomes. Here three days of observation identified a significant downward shift across followups in treated children's position relative to comparison children on the on task variable. Analyses based on two days of observation did not identify this shift.

These findings do not provide a clear answer as to whether or not two days of observation would be sufficient. On the one hand, the third day of observation did have a minimal additive effect. On the other hand, significant effects of the third day were found only for the on task variable, which had weak effects relative to the other variables in the study and could easily represent chance variation. This is a matter that warrants further investigation in sample sizes that would permit the use of more sophisticated statistical evaluation of the substantive effects of additional days of observation.

Information on longterm maintenance of treatment gains outside the classroom was not addressed in the current study. The treatment group in this study forms a subset of a larger group in which comprehensive evaluation of home maintenance of treatment effects up to two years posttreatment is ongoing. The current findings will be combined with clinic and home maintenance findings as they become available; unfortunately, the size of the current sample will continue to impose statistical and interpretive limitations. A larger scale PCIT treatment outcome study is also ongoing and it will include assessment of school generalization. It is hoped that sufficient sample size will be available in that project to address questions raised in this study such as incremental effects of

additional days of observation, differential outcome for
diagnostic subgroupings of disruptive behavior disorders,
effects of stimulant medication on longterm classroom
maintenance, and the nature of the association between
classroom behavioral maintenance and outcome in settings
other than the classroom.

PASSIVE CONSENT FORM

Dear Parent(s),

We are conducting a research project to learn more about the school behavior of young children. We want to know how children in regular and special preschool and elementary classrooms behave so that we can more effectively aid children referred to our Psychology Clinic because of school behavior problems. This work is important not only for the children with behavior problems, but for all children because one child's misbehavior often disrupts a whole classroom and interrupts everyone's learning.

In our study an observer will go into your child's classroom for about an hour and a half on three different days. This person will randomly select from two to ten children (depending on the size of the class) from the class roll book and will keep track of how many times those children obey the teacher or are disruptive in the classroom. The teacher may also be asked to complete three questionnaires about those children's classroom behavior and how they get along with other children. Children will not be identified by name so there will be no way that a child could be identified by our research records.

Although it is possible that having a new person in the classroom will distract the children from schoolwork, based

123

on our experience, this is not usually a problem. In fact, it is unlikely that a child will know that he or she is being observed. Our observer will sit in a far corner of the room and will not disrupt the classroom routine.

If you do **not** wish your child to be observed, please sign this form and return it to your child's teacher within five (5) school days. Children whose parents do not wish them to be observed will be removed from the class list from which children are randomly selected. Children whose parents do not return this form in five school days will be considered eligible for the study. If at a later date you decide that you do not want your child to participate, simply inform your child's teacher or contact Beverly Funderburk.

If you have any questions about this study, please contact the project director, Beverly Funderburk at (904) 395-0294 or (904) 372-6468. Thank you for your cooperation.

Beverly Funderburk, M.S.   Sheila Eyberg, Ph.D.

Doctoral Student   Professor
Dept. of Clinical and   Dept. of Clinical and
Health Psychology   Health Psychology

_____ <u>No</u>, I do not wish for my child to participate in this

study.

_____
(parent's signature)

**Note: You do not need to return this form if you agree for
your child to be included in the study.**

APPENDIX B

COMPARISON SUBJECT SELECTION FORM

Teacher _____ School _____

Please list the initials of all the boys in your class,
ranking each boy's behavior relative to the behavior of boys
in this class.

		fewest problems				most problems
1.	_____	1	2	3	4	5
2.	_____	1	2	3	4	5
3.	_____	1	2		4	5
4.	_____	1	2	3	4	5
5.	_____	1	2	3	4	5
6.	_____	1	2		4	5
7.	_____	1	2	3	4	5
8.	_____	1	2		4	5
9.	_____	1	2	3	4	5
10.	_____	1	2	3	4	5
11.	_____	1	2	3	4	5
12.	_____	1	2	3	4	5
13.	_____	1	2	3	4	5
14.	_____	1	2		4	5
15.	_____	1	2	3	4	5

To your knowledge, will any of the boys be absent
during the scheduled observation periods?

126

EYBERG CHILD BEHAVIOR INVENTORY

Rater's Name:

Relationship to Child:

Date of Rating:

Child's Name:

Child's Age:

Birthdate:

Directions: Below are a series of phrases that describe children's behavior. Please (1) circle the number describing how often the behavior currently occurs with your child (1=Never; 2 to 3 = Seldom; 4 = Sometimes; 5 to 6 = Often; 7 = Always), and (2) circle either "Y" (yes) or "N" (no) to indicate whether the behavior is currently a problem.

1.	Dawdles in getting dressed	1 2 3 4 5 6 7	Y	N
2.	Dawdles or lingers at mealtime	1 2 3 4 5 6 7	Y	N
3.	Has poor table manners	1 2 3 4 5 6 7	Y	N
4.	Refuses to eat food presented	1 2 3 4 5 6 7	Y	N
5.	Refuses to do chores when asked	1 2 3 4 5 6 7	Y	N
6.	Slow in getting ready for bed	1 2 3 4 5 6 7	Y	N
7.	Refuses to go to bed on time	1 2 3 4 5 6 7	Y	N

8. Does not obey house rules on   1 2 3 4 5 6 7   Y N
   his own

9. Refuses to obey until   1 2 3 4 5 6 7   Y N
   threatened with punishment

10. Acts defiant when told to   1 2 3 4 5 6 7   Y N
    do something

11. Argues with parents about   1 2 3 4 5 6 7   Y N
    rules

12. Gets angry when doesn't get   1 2 3 4 5 6 7   Y N
    his own way

13. Has temper tantrums   1 2 3 4 5 6 7   Y N

14. Sasses adults   1 2 3 4 5 6 7   Y N

15. Whines   1 2 3 4 5 6 7   Y N

16. Cries easily   1 2 3 4 5 6 7   Y N

17. Yells or screams   1 2 3 4 5 6 7   Y N

18. Hits parents   1 2 3 4 5 6 7   Y N

19. Destroys toys and other   1 2 3 4 5 6 7   Y N
    objects

20. Is careless with toys or   1 2 3 4 5 6 7   Y N
    other objects

21. Steals   1 2 3 4 5 6 7   Y N

22. Lies   1 2 3 4 5 6 7   Y N

23. Teases or provokes other   1 2 3 4 5 6 7   Y N
    children

24. Verbally fights with friends   1 2 3 4 5 6 7   Y N
    his own age

25. Verbally fights with sisters   1 2 3 4 5 6 7   Y N

and brothers

26. Physically fights with   1 2 3 4 5 6 7   Y   N

    friends his own age

27. Physically fights with   1 2 3 4 5 6 7   Y   N

    sisters and brothers

28. Constantly seeks attention   1 2 3 4 5 6 7   Y   N

29. Interrupts   1 2 3 4 5 6 7   Y   N

30. Is easily distracted   1 2 3 4 5 6 7   Y   N

31. Has short attention span   1 2 3 4 5 6 7   Y   N

32. Fails to finish tasks or   1 2 3 4 5 6 7   Y   N

    projects

33. Has difficulty entertaining   1 2 3 4 5 6 7   Y   N

    himself alone

34. Has difficulty concentrating   1 2 3 4 5 6 7   Y   N

    on one thing

35. Is overactive or restless   1 2 3 4 5 6 7   Y   N

36. Wets the bed   1 2 3 4 5 6 7   Y   N

REVISED CONNERS TEACHER RATING SCALE

Name of Child:

Date of Evaluation:

Grade:

Please answer all questions. Beside each item, indicate the degree of the problem by a check mark.

1 = Not at all

2 = Just a little

3 = Pretty much

4 = Very much

1.	Restless in the "squirmy" sense.	1	2	3	4
2.	Makes inappropriate noises when he shouldn't.	1	2	3	4
3.	Demands must be met immediately.	1	2	3	4
4.	Acts "smart" (impudent or sassy).	1	2	3	4
5.	Temper outbursts and unpredictable behavior.	1	2	3	4
6.	Overly sensitive to criticism.	1	2	3	4
7.	Distractibility or attention span a problem.	1	2	3	4
8.	Disturbs other children.	1	2	3	4
9.	Daydreams.	1	2	3	4
10.	Pouts and sulks.	1	2	3	4

11. Mood changes quickly and drastically. 1 2 3 4

12. Quarrelsome. 1 2 3 4

13. Submissive attitude toward authority. 1 2 3 4

14. Restless, always "up and on the go." 1 2 3 4

15. Excitable, impulsive. 1 2 3 4

16. Excessive demands for teacher's attention. 1 2 3 4

17. Appears to be unaccepted by group. 1 2 3 4

18. Appears to be easily led by other children. 1 2 3 4

19. No sense of fair play. 1 2 3 4

20. Appears to lack leadership. 1 2   4

21. Fails to finish things that he started. 1 2 3 4

22. Childish and immature. 1 2 3 4

23. Denies mistakes or blames others. 1 2 3 4

24. Does not get along well with other children. 1 2 3 4

25. Uncooperative with classmates. 1 2 3 4

26. Easily frustrated in efforts. 1 2 3 4

27. Uncooperative with teacher. 1 2 3 4

28. Difficulty in learning. 1 2 3 4

SUTTER-EYBERG STUDENT BEHAVIOR INVENTORY

Rater's Name:

Relationship to Child:

Date of Rating:

Child's Name:

Child's Age:

Birthdate:

Directions: Below are a series of phrases that describe children's behavior. Please (1) circle the number describing how often the behavior currently occurs with this student (1=Never; 2 to 3 = Seldom; 4 = Sometimes; 5 to 6 = Often; 7 = Always), and (2) circle either "Y" (yes) or "N" (no) to indicate whether the behavior is currently a problem.

1. Dawdles in obeying rules or instructions   1 2 3 4 5 6 7   Y   N

2. Argues with teachers about rules or instructions   1 2 3 4 5 6 7   Y   N

3. Has difficulty accepting criticism or correction   1 2 3 4 5 6 7   Y   N

4. Does not obey school rules on his/her own   1 2 3 4 5 6 7   Y   N

5. Refuses to obey until   1 2 3 4 5 6 7   Y   N
threatened with punishment

6. Gets angry when doesn't   1 2 3 4 5 6 7   Y   N
get his/her own way

7. Acts defiant when told to   1 2 3 4 5 6 7   Y   N
do something

8. Has temper tantrums   1 2 3 4 5 6 7   Y   N

9. Sasses teacher(s)   1 2 3 4 5 6 7   Y   N

10. Whines   1 2 3 4 5 6 7   Y   N

11. Cries   1 2 3 4 5 6 7   Y   N

12. Pouts   1 2 3 4 5 6 7   Y   N

13. Yells or screams   1 2 3 4 5 6 7   Y   N

14. Hits teacher(s)   1 2 3 4 5 6 7   Y   N

15. Is careless with books   1 2 3 4 5 6 7   Y   N
and other objects

16. Destroys books and other   1 2 3 4 5 6 7   Y   N
objects

17. Steals   1 2 3 4 5 6 7   Y   N

18. Lies   1 2 3 4 5 6 7   Y   N

19. Makes noises in class   1 2 3 4 5 6 7   Y   N

20. Teases or provokes other   1 2 3 4 5 6 7   Y   N
students

21. Acts bossy with other   1 2 3 4 5 6 7   Y   N
students

22. Verbally fights with other   1 2 3 4 5 6 7   Y   N
students

23. Physically fights with other   1 2 3 4 5 6 7   Y   N
    students

24. Demands teacher attention   1 2 3 4 5 6 7   Y   N

25. Interrupts teachers   1 2 3 4 5 6 7   Y   N

26. Interrupts other students   1 2 3 4 5 6 7   Y   N

27. Has difficulty entering   1 2 3 4 5 6 7   Y   N
    groups

28. Has difficulty sharing   1 2 3 4 5 6 7   Y   N
    materials

29. Is uncooperative in group   1 2 3 4 5 6 7   Y   N
    activities

30. Blames others for problem   1 2 3 4 5 6 7   Y   N
    behaviors

31. Is easily distracted   1 2 3 4 5 6 7   Y   N

32. Has difficulty staying on   1 2 3 4 5 6 7   Y   N
    task

33. Acts frustrated with   1 2 3 4 5 6 7   Y   N
    difficult tasks

34. Fails to finish tasks or   1 2 3 4 5 6 7   Y   N
    projects

35. Impulsive, acts before thinking   1 2 3 4 5 6 7   Y   N

36. Is overactive or restless   1 2 3 4 5 6 7   Y   N

WALKER-McCONNELL SCALE OF SOCIAL COMPETENCE
AND SCHOOL ADJUSTMENT: A SOCIAL SKILLS
RATING SCALE FOR TEACHERS

I. Student Demographic Information

Date Administered:

Classroom Type: Regular   Resource   Self-contained

Student Name:

Teacher:

Sex: M   F   Age: Years _____   Months _____

II. Rating Instructions

Please read each item below carefully and rate the
child's behavioral status in relation to it. If you have
not observed the child displaying a particular skill or
behavioral competency defined by an item, check 1,
indicating Never. If the child exhibits the skill at a high
rate of occurrence, check 5, for Frequently. If the child's
frequency is in between these two extremes, please check 2,
3, or 4, indicating your best estimate of its rate of
occurrence.

Please answer each item. DO NOT MARK BETWEEN THE NUMBERS ON
THE RATING SCALE. Check one of the numbers from 1-5 to
indicate your frequency estimate.

Numbers in parentheses to the left of the item number
represent the subscale for that particular item.

III. Items and Rating Formats

(2) 1. Other children seek child out   1..2..3..4..5
         to involve her/him in activities.

(2) 2. Changes activities with peers   1..2..3..4..5
         to permit continued interaction.

(3) 3. Uses free time appropriately.   1..2..3..4..5

(2) 4. Shares laughter with peers.   1..2..3..4..5

(1) 5. Shows sympathy for others.   1..2..3..4..5

(2) 6. Makes friends easily with   1..2..3..4..5
         other children.

(3) 7. Has good work habits, e.g., is   1..2..3..4..5
         organized, makes efficient use
         of class time, etc.

(2) 8. Asks questions that request   1..2..3..4..5
         information about someone or
         something.

(1) 9. Compromises with peers when   1..2..3..4..5
         situation calls for it.

(1) 10. Responds to teasing or name   1..2..3..4..5
         calling by ignoring, changing
         the subject, or some other
         constructive means.

(2) 11. Spends recess and free time   1..2..3..4..5
         interacting with peers.

(1) 12. Accepts constructive criticism   1..2..3..4..5
         from peers without becoming angry.

(2) 13. Plays or talks with peers for   1..2..3..4..5
         extended periods of time.

(2) 14. Voluntarily provides assistance   1..2..3..4..5
         to peers who require it.

(2) 15. Assumes leadership role in peer   1..2..3..4..5
         activities.

(1) 16. Is sensitive to the needs of others. 1..2..3..4..5

(2) 17. Initiates conversations(s) with   1..2..3..4..5
         peers in informal situations.

(1) 18. Expresses anger appropriately,   1..2..3..4..5
         e.g., reacts to situation without
         becoming violent or destructive.

(3) 19. Listens carefully to teacher   1..2..3..4..5
         instructions and directions for
         assignments.

(3) 20. Answers or attempts to answer a   1..2..3..4..5
         questions when called on by the
         teacher.

(3) 21. Displays independent study skills,   1..2..3..4..5
         e.g., can work adequately with
         minimum teacher support.

(1) 22. Appropriately copes with aggression 1..2..3..4..5
         from others, e.g., tries to avoid
         a fight, walks away, seeks assistance,

defends self.

(3) 23. Responds to conventional behavior 1..2..3..4..5
management techniques, e.g.,
praise, reprimands, time-out.

(1) 24. Cooperates with peers in group 1..2..3..4..5
activities or situations.

(2) 25. Interacts with a number of 1..2..3..4..5
different peers.

(1) 26. Uses physical contact with peers 1..2..3..4..5
appropriately.

(3) 27. Responds to requests promptly. 1..2..3..4..5

(1) 28. Listens while others are speaking, 1..2..3..4..5
e.g., as in circle or sharing time.

(1) 29. Controls temper. 1..2..3..4..5

(2) 30. Compliments others regarding 1..2..3..4..5
personal attributes, e.g.,
appearance, special skills, etc.

(1) 31. Can accept not getting her/his 1..2..3..4..5
own way.

(2) 32. Is socially perceptive, e.g., reads 1..2..3..4..5
social situations accurately.

(3) 33. Attends to assigned tasks. 1..2..3..4..5

(2) 34. Plays games and activities at 1..2..3..4..5
recess skillfully.

(2) 35. Keeps conversation with peers going. 1..2..3..4..5

(1) 36. Finds another way to play when   1..2..3..4..5
        requests to join others are refused.

(1) 37. Is considerate of the feelings of   1..2..3..4..5
        others.

(2) 38. Maintains eye contact when speaking   1..2..3..4..5
        or being spoken to.

(1) 39. Gains peers' attention in an   1..2..3..4..5
        appropriate manner.

(1) 40. Accepts suggestions and assistance   1..2..3..4..5
        from peers.

(2) 41. Invites peers to play or share   1..2..3..4..5
        activities.

(3) 42. Does seatwork assignments as   1..2..3..4..5
        directed.

(3) 43. Produces work of acceptable   1..2..3..4..5
        quality given her/his skills
        level.

BODIFORD-MCNEIL CLASSROOM CODING SYSTEM

There are three behavior categories that must be coded
for each child: 1) Appropriate Behavior vs. Oppositional
Behavior, 2) Comply vs. Noncomply vs. Unsure/No Command
Given, and 3) On Task vs. Off Task vs. Not Applicable. This
is a "forced choice" system in that the coder must enter
only one mark in each of the three categories. Coding is
done using an interval sampling procedure. The coder
observes the target child for a 10-second time interval then
makes one mark in each of the three categories. The coder
is given ten seconds to mark the categories before the next
10-second observation interval begins. The coder will
listen to an audiotape (using an ear jack) which will
deliver prompts to "start" and "stop" for each observation
interval.

Definitions of Behavioral Categories

Appropriate Behavior - the absence of all Oppositional
Behaviors. Behavior must be appropriate for the entire 10-
second interval. If unsure as to whether behavior is
appropriate or oppositional, code Appropriate Behavior

Oppositional Behavior - The following behaviors are
coded as Oppositional Behaviors because they are annoying or

disruptive to the target child, the teacher, or other
children:

a) <u>Whining</u> - Words uttered by the child in a slurring,
nasal, high-pitched, falsetto voice.

b) <u>Crying</u> - Inarticulate utterances of distress (audible
weeping) which may or may not be accompanied by tears.

c) <u>Yelling</u> - Loud screeching, screaming, shouting, or
crying. The sound must be loud enough so that it is clearly
above the intensity of normal indoor conversation. Not
coded during outdoor recess observations.

d) <u>Tantruming</u> - Any combination of whining, yelling, crying,
hitting, and/or kicking.

e) <u>Destructiveness</u> - Behaviors in which the child damages or
destroys an object or attempts or threatens to damage
an object or injure a person. Do not code if it is
appropriate within the context of the play situation,
e.g., ramming cars in a car crash. Examples of
aggression toward persons include fighting, kicking,
slapping, hitting, or grabbing an object roughly away
from another person, or threatening to do any of the
preceding.

f) <u>Negativism</u> - A verbal or nonverbal negative behavior.
May be scored when the child makes a statement in which the
verbal message may be neutral but which is delivered in a
tone of voice that conveys an attitude of "don't bug me, or
"don't bother me." Negativism may be expressed in a
derogatory, uncomplimentary, or angry manner. Also

included are defeatist statements such as "I give up,"
contradictions of what another person says (e.g.,
teacher says: "Johnny did a nice job," child says: "He did
not."), and teasing or mocking behaviors or verbalizations.

g) Pathological Self-Stimulation - Repetitive behavior that
may be harmful and interfere with a child's ability to
attend or complete a task. Examples of pathological
self-stimulation include head-banging, thumb-sucking,
and masturbation.

h) Demanding Attention - Includes repetitive verbal and
nonverbal requests for attention from the teacher or other
students (e.f., "Call on me! Call on me! Call on me!").
Other behavior that are coded in this category included
making faces, making disruptive noises, repetitively tugging
on teacher's sleeve, tapping neighbor on the shoulder,
waving arms in air, passing notes to another child, and
clowning.

i) High-Rate Behavior - Any very physically active,
repetitive behavior that has been carried on sufficiently
long that it has become disruptive to either the target
child or others. Examples include kicking a child's chair
repeatedly, drumming on the table loudly, and spinning a
pencil on the desk.

j) Talking Out of Order - Any verbalization made in a
situation in which the children are clearly expected
to be silent unless asked to speak. Talking Out of
Order includes whispering to a neighbor, answering a

question not directed toward the target child, talking, singing or humming to oneself, and calling out to another child.

k) <u>Being Out of Area</u> - Coded when the target child without permission leaves the area that he is clearly expected to stay in. Examples include standing up when rest of class is seated, leaving desk, approaching the teacher without permission, playing with an attractive toy that is not in the work area the child is supposed to be in. When coding, be certain that the out of area behavior is inappropriate for the context or classroom norms (e.g., in some classrooms the teacher may not be disturbed if the child spontaneously walks to the teacher's desk if he obviously needs help on a math problem).

l) <u>Cheating</u> - Child borrows another child's work when such behavior is clearly not allowed. Examples include looking at another child's paper during a spelling quiz and copying another child's work.

<u>Comply</u> - The target child obeys, begins to obey, or attempts to obey (within 5 seconds) of a direct or indirect teacher command. The command can be one directed toward the target child individually or to a group of children that includes the target child. To be coded, the command must be given during the 10-second observation interval. If the command is given near the end of the 10-second observation interval, continue to watch for 5 seconds to determine whether the child complies.

Noncomply - Target child makes no movement toward obeying a direct or indirect teacher command during a 5-second period following the command.

Unsure/No Command - This category is coded when the observer is unsure about whether the child obeyed the command, or no command was in effect during the 10-second observation interval. Examples of commands that the coder is likely to be unsure about include: "All children who got stars last week come to the front of the room," "Say the word h-a-p-p-y" (target child's back is turned to observer), "If you haven't finished your worksheet, do it now" (observer is sitting at a distance and can't tell whether target child's paper is finished).

On Task - The child is considered to be On Task if he is (a) attending to the material and the task, (b) making appropriate motor responses (e.g. writing, computing, pasting), or (c) asking for assistance (where appropriate) in an acceptable manner. Interacting with the teacher or classmates about academic matters or listening to teacher instructions and directions are considered to be On Task behaviors. To be coded as On Task, the child must remain on task for the full 10-second observation interval.

Off Task - Coded if at any point during the 10-second interval the child is engaging in behavior that does not meet the definition for On Task behavior. Examples of Off Task include failure to attend to or work on the assigned task, breaking classroom rules (out of seat, talking out, disturbing others, etc.), laying head on desk passively when there is a task to complete, and daydreaming. If the child is in time out during the observation interval, he or she is automatically coded as Off Task.

Not applicable - Coded when there is no readily identifiable task that the children are expected to perform. Examples of Not Applicable activities include free play and unstructured recess time.

APPENDIX H

REVISED CLASSROOM CODING SYSTEM

Three behavior categories are coded for each child: 1)
Appropriate Behavior vs. Oppositional Behavior vs. Unsure,
2) Comply vs. Noncomply vs. Unsure/No Command Given/No Opp,
and 3) On Task vs. Off task vs. Not Applicable. This is a
"forced choice" system in that the coder must enter only one
mark in each of the three categories (No mark required for
Appropriate; only oppositional behaviors marked in this
category). Coding is continuous within ten second
intervals. There will be a 15-second break after every
minute of coding. On Task behavior is coded in 10-second
intervals, with the child required to remain on task for the
entire interval to be considered on task. The coder will
listen to an audiotape (using an ear jack) which will
deliver prompts for the observation intervals.

Definitions of Behavioral Categories

Appropriate Behavior - the absence of all Oppositional
Behaviors. Behavior must be appropriate for the entire 10-
second interval. If unsure as to whether behavior was
appropriate or oppositional (e.g., you hear a yell but are
not sure whether the observed child or the child beside him
yelled), code as unsure ("?").

146

Oppositional Behavior - The following behaviors are
coded as Oppositional Behaviors because they may be
annoying or disruptive to the target child, the teacher, or
other children:

Whining - Coherent **words** uttered by the child in a slurring,
nasal, high-pitched, falsetto voice.

Crying - Inarticulate utterances of distress (audible
weeping) which may or may not be accompanied by tears.

Yelling - Loud screeching, screaming, or shouting. The
sound must be loud enough so that it is clearly above
the intensity of normal indoor conversation. Not coded
during outdoor recess observations.

Tantruming - Any combination of whining, yelling crying,
hitting and/or kicking.

Destructiveness - Behaviors in which the child damages or
destroys an object or attempts or threatens to damage
an object or injure a person. Do not code if it is
appropriate within the context of the play situation,
e.g., ramming cars in a car crash. Examples of
aggression toward persons include fighting, kicking,
slapping, hitting, or grabbing an object roughly away
from another person, or threatening to do any of the
preceding.

Negativism - Verbal or nonverbal negative behavior. May
be scored when the child makes a statement in which the
verbal message may be neutral but which is delivered in a
tone of voice that conveys an attitude of "don't bother me."

Negativism may be expressed in a derogatory, uncomplimentary, or angry manner. Also included are defeatist statements such as "I give up," contradictions of what another person says (e.g., teacher says: "Johnny did a nice job," child says: "He did not."), and teasing or mocking behaviors or verbalizations. "Pouting" facial expressions are also included, but not audible whines.

Pathological Self-Stimulation - Repetitive physical movements involving only the child's body and not other objects that interfere with a child's ability to attend or complete a task. Examples of pathological self-stimulation include head-banging, thumb-sucking, and masturbation.

Disruptive Behavior - Any very physically active, repetitive behavior that has been carried on sufficiently long that it has become disruptive to either the target child or others. Examples include kicking a child's chair repeatedly, drumming on the table loudly, clowning, making funny noises, and spinning a pencil on the desk. Also includes nonverbal demands for attention such as repetitively tapping neighbor on the shoulder, passing notes, or tugging on a teacher's arm.

Talking Out of Order - Any coherent verbalizations made in a situation in which the children are clearly expected to be silent unless asked to speak. Talking out of order includes whispering to a neighbor, answering a question not directed toward the target child, talking or singing to oneself, and calling out to another child. Disruptive verbal demands for attention (e.g., calling to a child or teacher across the room) are coded even during times when quiet talking is permitted if it is outside the appropriate range.

Being Out of Area - Coded when the target child without permission leaves the area that he is clearly expected to stay in. Examples include standing up when rest of class is seated, leaving desk, approaching the teacher without permission, playing with an attractive toy that is not in the work area the child is supposed to be in. When coding, be certain that the out of area behavior is inappropriate for the context or classroom norms (e.g., in some classrooms the teacher may not be disturbed if the child spontaneously walks to the teacher's desk if he obviously needs help on a math problem).

Cheating - Child borrows another child's work when such behavior is clearly not allowed. Examples include looking at another child's paper during a spelling quiz and copying another child's work.

Comply - The target child obeys, begins to obey, or attempts to obey within 5 seconds of a direct or indirect teacher command. The command can be one directed toward the target child individually or to a group of children that includes the target child. To be coded, the command must be given within 5-seconds of the start of a one-minute coding period.

Noncomply - Target child makes no movement toward obeying a direct or indirect teacher command during a 5-second period following the command.

Unsure/No Command - No command is coded when the observer is unsure about whether the child obeyed the command, or no command was issued during the 10-second observation interval. Examples of commands that the coder is likely to be unsure about whether the child obeyed include: "All child who got stars last week come to the front of the room," "Say the word h-a-p-p-y" (target child's back is turned to observer), "If you haven't finished your worksheet, do it now" (observer is sitting at a distance and cannot tell whether target child's paper is finished). No opportunity commands (repeated rapidly without opportunity for compliance; or commands which appear to be above the child's level of understanding) are not coded. Negative commands (Do not . . .) are only coded in the case where a child is actively involved in a physical activity which the teacher commands him to stop - making it clearly observable to the coder whether the child complies or noncomplies within a 5-second interval.

On Task - The child is considered to be On Task if he is (a) attending to the material and the task, (b) making appropriate motor responses (e.g., writing, computing, pasting), or (c) asking for assistance (where appropriate) in an acceptable manner. Interacting with the teacher or classmates about academic matters or listening to teacher instructions and directions are also considered to be On Task behaviors. To be coded as On Task, the child must remain on task for the full 10-second observation interval.

Off Task - Coded if at any point during the 10-second interval the child is engaging in behavior that does not meet the definition for On Task behavior. Examples of Off Task include failure to attend to or work on the assigned task, breaking classroom rules (out of seat, talking out, disturbing others, etc.), laying head on desk passively when there is a task to complete, and daydreaming.

Not applicable - Scored when there is no readily identifiable task that the children are expected to perform. Examples of Not Applicable activities include free play and unstructured recess time.

11/89 revision/Funderburk

RESEARCH PARTICIPANT CONTACT FORM

Child's Name _____

Parent(s) Name _____

    Address   _____

                _____

    Home Phone: _____ Daytime Phone:

    Please list the name, address, and phone number of three relatives or friends who will always know how to contact you.

Name: _____

    Address _____

            _____

    Home Phone _____ Daytime Phone

Name: _____

    Address _____

            _____

    Home Phone _____ Daytime Phone

Name: _____

    Address _____

            _____

    Home Phone _____ Daytime Phone

I, _____, give my permission for the above named persons to be contacted by members of the Parent-Child Interaction Therapy research team. Such contact will be limited to seeking information on how we could locate you for follow-up visits in case you should change your address or phone number.

_____   _____

(signature)   (date)

_____   _____

(witness)   (date)

APPENDIX J

INFORMED CONSENT TO PARTICIPATE IN RESEARCH

J. HILLIS MILLER HEALTH CENTER

UNIVERSITY OF FLORIDA

GAINESVILLE, FLORIDA 32610

You are being asked to volunteer as a participant in a
research study. This form is designed to provide you with
information about this study and to answer any of your
questions.

1. TITLE OF RESEARCH STUDY

        Parent-Child Interaction Training with

        Behavior Problem Children: Maintenance of

        Treatment Effects in the School Setting

 2. PROJECT DIRECTOR

    Name: Beverly W. Funderburk, M.S.

    Telephone Number: 372-6468 (home)

                       395-0294 (Psychology Clinic)

3. THE PURPOSE OF THE RESEARCH

    The purpose of this study is to evaluate the long-term
effectiveness of Parent-Child Interaction Therapy on your
child's school behavior. Initial research indicates that

this treatment is effective in decreasing school behavior problems for most children. This study will evaluate whether behavioral improvements seen in school at the end of the treatment program continue during the next school year. Specific classroom behaviors that will be evaluated include obeying teacher instructions, disruptive behaviors (such as hitting, yelling, and sassing), attention span, and getting along with other children.

4. PROCEDURES FOR THIS RESEARCH

Families who completed the original school study will be invited to participate. Children in the study will be evaluated at school approximately eight months after the end of treatment and again approximately fourteen months after treatment. Several nontreated control children will again be randomly selected from your child's classroom. The control children and their parents will not be informed that your child has been in treatment. All participating children will be observed for two hours on three different days while going about the normal classroom routine. This will provide information about how well the children obey their teachers and get along with their classmates. The teacher will also be asked to rate the classroom behavior of each child. This will not require that your child be taken out of the classroom.

5. POTENTIAL RISKS OR DISCOMFORTS

If you wish to discuss these or any other discomforts

you may experience, you may call the Project Director listed in #2 of this form.

All of the procedures used in this study are commonly used by psychologists and will pose minimal risk or discomfort to your child. However, it is possible that your child may be distracted from ongoing classroom activities by the presence of observers in the classroom. However, the observers will sit at the back of the classroom and be as non-distracting as possible. It is likely that your child will not realize he or she is being observed.

6. POTENTIAL BENEFITS TO YOUR OR TO OTHERS

Based on our experience, informing teachers of a child's participation in a treatment program often has a positive effect on the relationship with the teacher, as does contact with members of the PCIT treatment team.

Parents who request information on the school evaluations will be given feedback.

7. ALTERNATIVE TREATMENT OR PROCEDURES, IF APPLICABLE

If you choose not to participate in this followup study, you will still be eligible for followup consultations and/or future treatment through this clinic.

APPENDIX K

INFORMATION RELEASE FORM FOR PERMISSION TO CONTACT SCHOOL

PSYCHOLOGY CLINIC
Department of Clinical and Health Psychology
UNIVERSITY OF FLORIDA

Box J-165
Gainesville, FL 32610
Shands Teaching Hospitals and Clinics
Phone: (904) 395-0294

CONSENT FOR RELEASE OF INFORMATION

I hereby authorize the Psychology Clinic of Shands Teaching
Hospital, University of Florida, to release and/or exchange
any and all information which they possess relating to my
child's examinations and illnesses, including psychiatric
and/or psychological information which may be part of the
medical record, to:

_____
(Name of child's teacher, principal, and/or counselor)

_____

_____
(Name and address of school)

_____   _____
Signature of Parent or Guardian   Date
(Required if the Patient is under
the age of 18)

_____   _____
Signature of Witness   Date

APPENDIX L

ADDITIONAL INFORMATION FORM

Teacher _____ School _____

You have been asked to complete ratings on four children
from your classroom. Please answer the following questions
about these children:

To your knowledge have any of these children received
treatment for behavior problems? Please write their
initials: _____

Do you feel that any of these children are in need of
professional treatment for behavior problems? Please write
their initials: _____

To your knowledge have any of these children been
referred for special educational services? Please write
their initials:_____

During the classroom observations, did any of the
children show behavior that is very different from their
usual behavior (example: a normally active child being quiet
and drowsy due to a cold). Please list the initials of
children whose behavior was atypical and briefly describe
how it was different from usual: _____

_____

_____

PLOTS OF INDIVIDUAL SUBJECTS' SCORES PER VARIABLE

```
SESBI Prob.-------------+-----------------+-----------------+---
 36 +                   |                 |                   +
 35 +                   |                 |                   +
 34 +                   |                 |                   +
 33 +                   |                 |                   +
 32 +                   |                 |                   +
 31 +                   |                 |                   +
 30 +   I               |                 |             C     +
 29 +                   |                 |                   +
 28 +                   |                 |                   +
 27 +   C               |                 |                   +
 26 +   E K             |                 |                   +
 25 +                   |                 |                   +
 24 +                   E                 |                   +
 23 +   J               |                 |           I G     +
 22 +                   |                 |             B     +
 21 +                   |                 A                   +
 20 +   B               |                 I                   +
 19 +                   |                 |             A     +
 18 +                   |                 |                   +
 17 +   D               |                 J                   +
 16 +                   I                 |                   +
 15 +   A H             C                 |                   +
 14 +   F               |                 |             D     +
 13 +                   F                 B             J     +
 12 +                   |                 |                   +
 11 +   G L             |                 |             E     +
 10 +                   |                 |                   +
  9 +                   J                 |                   +
  8 +                   A                 |                   +
  7 +                   B                 |                   +
  6 +                   |                 D             K     +
  5 +                   |                 |                   +
  4 +                   |                 F             H     +
  3 +                 G D                 C             F     +
  2 +                   |                 |                   +
  1 +                   H                 L                   +
  0 +                   K                 KH                  +
   ---+-----------------+-----------------+-----------------+---
      1                 2                 3                 4
                   missing: L        missing: E,G        missing: L
```

TIME

Note: Underline indicates subject on stimulant medication

SESBI PROBLEM SCORES BY SUBJECT ACROSS TIME

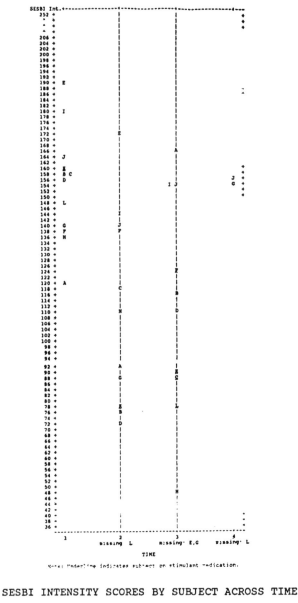

SESBI INTENSITY SCORES BY SUBJECT ACROSS TIME

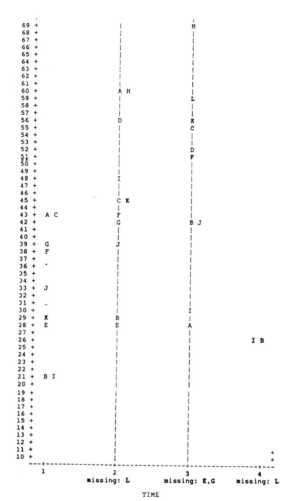

Note: Underline indicates subject on stimulant medication.

WALKER-MCCONNELL TEACHER PREFERRED BEHAVIOR SCORES
BY SUBJECT ACROSS TIME

TIME

Note: Underline indicates subject on stimulant medication.

WALKER-MCCONNELL PEER PREFERRED BEHAVIOR SCORES BY SUBJECT ACROSS TIME

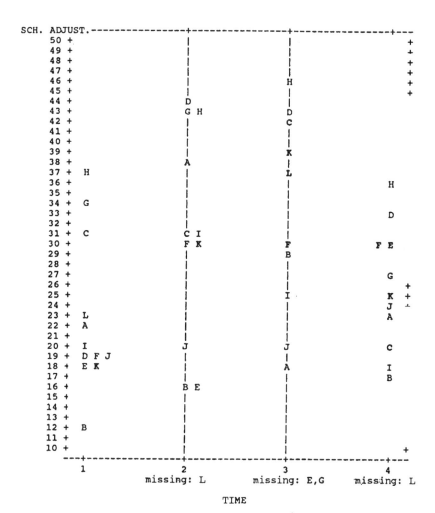

```
SCH. ADJUST. -------------------+-------------------+-------------------+---
    50 +                        |                   |                      +
    49 +                        |                   |                      ⊥
    48 +                        |                   |                      +
    47 +                        |                   |                      +
    46 +                        |                   H                      +
    45 +                        |                   |                      +
    44 +                        D                   |
    43 +                        G H                 D
    42 +                        |                   C
    41 +                        |                   |
    40 +                        |                   |
    39 +                        |                   K
    38 +                        A                   |
    37 +   H                    |                   L
    36 +                        |                   |              H
    35 +                        |                   |
    34 +   G                    |                   |              D
    33 +                        |                   |
    32 +                        |                   |
    31 +   C                    C I                 |
    30 +                        F K                 F            F E
    29 +                        |                   B
    28 +                        |                   |
    27 +                        |                   |              G
    26 +                        |                   |                 +
    25 +                        |                   I              K  +
    24 +                        |                   |              J  ⊥
    23 +   L                    |                   |              A
    22 +   A                    |                   |
    21 +                        |                   |
    20 +   I                    J                   J              C
    19 +   D F J                |                   |
    18 +   E K                  |                   A              I
    17 +                        |                   |              B
    16 +                        B E                 |
    15 +                        |                   |
    14 +                        |                   |
    13 +                        |                   |
    12 +   B                    |                   |
    11 +                        |                   |
    10 +                        |                   |                 +
   ---+-------------------+-------------------+-------------------+---
       1                   2                   3                   4
                     missing: L          missing: E,G        missing: L
                                   TIME
```

Note: Underline indicates subject on stimulant medication.

WALKER-MCCONNELL SCHOOL ADJUSTMENT SCORES BY SUBJECT ACROSS TIME

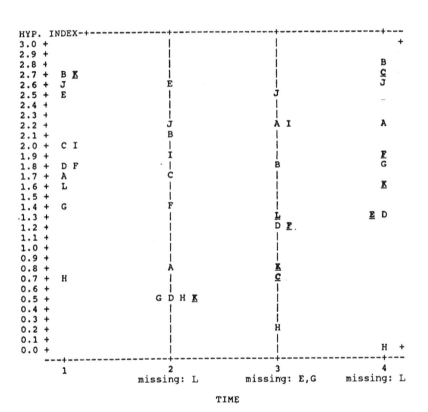

Note: Underline indicates subject on stimulant medication.

RCTRS HYPERACTIVITY INDEX SCORES BY SUBJECT ACROSS TIME

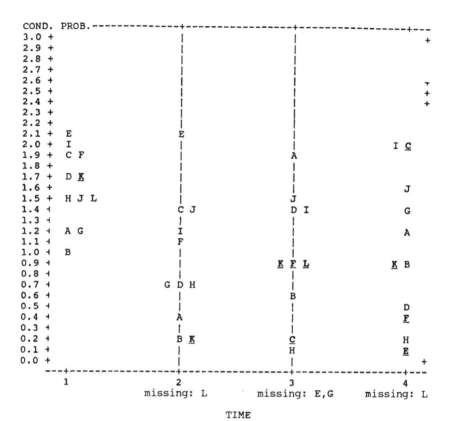

```
COND. PROB. ------------------+------------------+------------------+---
3.0 +                         |                  |                      +
2.9 +                         |                  |
2.8 +                         |                  |
2.7 +                         |                  |
2.6 +                         |                  |                      ⊤
2.5 +                         |                  |                      +
2.4 +                         |                  |                      +
2.3 +                         |                  |
2.2 +                         |                  |
2.1 +   E                     E                  |
2.0 +   I                     |                  |                  I C
1.9 +   C F                   |                  A
1.8 +                         |                  |
1.7 +   D K                   |                  |
1.6 +                         |                  |                      J
1.5 +   H J L                 |                  J
1.4 ⊣                         C J                D I                    G
1.3 ⊣                         |                  |
1.2 ⊣   A G                   I                  |                      A
1.1 ⊣                         F                  |
1.0 ⊣   B                     |                  |
0.9 ⊣                         |            K F L                    K B
0.8 ⊣                         |                  |
0.7 ⊣                       G D H                |
0.6 ⊣                         |                  B
0.5 ⊣                         |                  |                      D
0.4 ⊣                         A                  |                      F
0.3 ⊣                         |                  |
0.2 +                         B K                C                      H
0.1 +                         |                  H                      E
0.0 +                         |                  |                      +
    ---+------------------+------------------+------------------+---
       1                  2                  3                  4
                    missing: L      missing: E,G      missing: L

                            TIME
```

Note: Underline indicates subject on stimulant medication.

RCTRS CONDUCT PROBLEM FACTOR SCORES BY SUBJECT ACROSS TIME

```
INATT-PASS.---------------+-----------------+-----------------+---
3.0 +                     |                 |                       +
2.9 +                     |                 |
2.8 +                     |                 |
2.7 +  J                  |                 |                   A   +
2.6 +                     |                 B J                 C   +
2.5 +                     |                 |                       +
2.4 +  E K                |                 |
2.3 +                     |                 |
2.2 +                     |                 |
2.1 +  B                  B                 A                   J
2.0 +                     J                 |
1.9 +                     E                 |               G B
1.8 +                     |                 |
1.7 +                     |                 |
1.6 +  L                  |                 |
1.5 +  C                  |                 |           I F K E
1.4 +                     |                 |
1.3 +                     |                 |
1.2 +  G                  |                 F
1.1 +  A D F              C F               I
1.0 +                     |                 L
0.9 +                     |                 K                   D
0.8 +                     |                 |
0.7 +  H I                A I               |
0.6 +                     |                 D
0.5 +                     K                 |
0.4 +                     |                 |
0.3 +                     |                 |
0.2 +                     H                 C H                 H
0.1 +                     D G               |
0.0 +                     |                 |
   ---+-----------------+-----------------+-----------------+---
      1                 2                 3                 4
                  missing: L        missing: E,G        missing: L

                              TIME

    Note: Underline indicates subject on stimulant medication.


   RCTRS INATTENTIVE-PASSIVE FACTOR SCORES BY SUBJECT ACROSS TIME
```

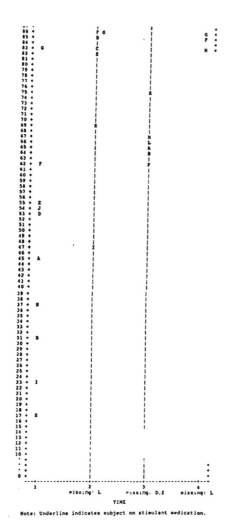

Note: Underline indicates subject on stimulant medication.

PLOT OF COMPLIANCE PERCENTAGES BY SUBJECT ACROSS TIME

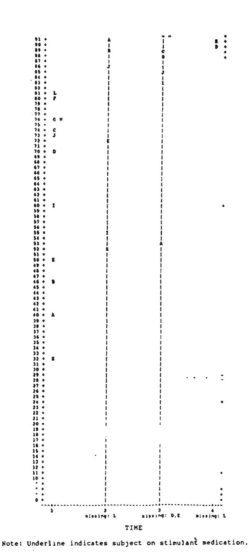

TIME

Note: Underline indicates subject on stimulant medication.

APPROPRIATE BEHAVIOR PERCENTAGES BY SUBJECT ACROSS TIME

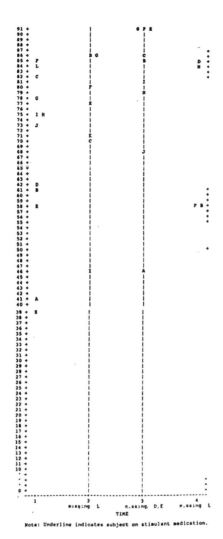

Note: Underline indicates subject on stimulant medication.

ON TASK BEHAVIOR PERCENTAGES BY SUBJECT ACROSS TIME

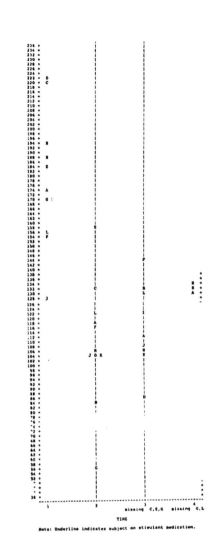

ECBI INTENSITY SCORES BY SUBJECT ACROSS TIME

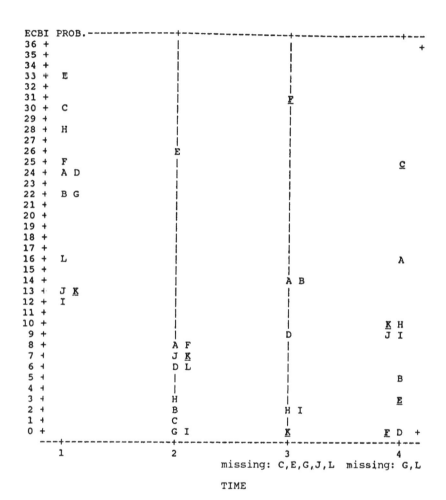

```
ECBI PROB. -------------+---------------+---------------+---
36 +                    |               |                 +
35 +                    |               |
34 +                    |               |
33 +  E                 |               |
32 +                    |               |
31 +                    |               F
30 +  C                 |               |
29 +                    |               |
28 +  H                 |               |
27 +                    |               |
26 +                  E |               |
25 +  F                 |               |                 C
24 +  A D               |               |
23 +                    |               |
22 +  B G               |               |
21 +                    |               |
20 +                    |               |
19 +                    |               |
18 +                    |               |
17 +                    |               |
16 +  L                 |               |                 A
15 +                    |               |
14 +                    |             A B
13 +  J K               |               |
12 +  I                 |               |
11 +                    |               |
10 +                    |               |               K H
 9 +                    |             D               J I
 8 +                  A F               |
 7 +                  J K               |
 6 +                  D L               |
 5 +                    |               |                 B
 4 +                    |               |
 3 +                  H |               |                 E
 2 +                  B |             H I
 1 +                  C |               |
 0 +                  G I             K               F D  +
   ---+----------------+---------------+---------------+---
      1                2               3               4
                          missing: C,E,G,J,L  missing: G,L
                          TIME
```

Note: Underline indicates subject on stimulant medication.

ECBI PROBLEM SCORES BY SUBJECT ACROSS TIME

REFERENCES

Abikoff, H., Gittelman, R. & Klein D. F. (1980). Classroom
observation code for hyperactive children: A
replication of validity. Journal of Consulting and
Clinical Psychology, 48, 555-565.

Abikoff, H., Gittelman-Klein, R., & Klein, D. F. (1977).
Validation of a classroom observational code for
hyperactive children. Journal of Consulting and
Clinical Psychology, 45, 772-783.

American Psychiatric Association (1987). Diagnostic and
statistical manual of mental disorders (3rd Ed.).
Washington, DC: Author.

Aragona, J. A., & Eyberg, S. M. (1981). Neglected children:
Mother's report of child behavior problems and
observed verbal behavior. Child Development, 52, 596-
602.

Atwater, J. B., & Morris, E. K. (1988). Teachers'
instructions and children's compliance in preschool
classrooms: A descriptive analysis. Journal of
Applied Behavior Analysis, 21, 157-167.

Bakeman, R., & Gottman, T. M. (1986). Observing
interaction: An introduction to sequential analysis.
New York: Cambridge University Press.

Barkley, R. A., Fischer, M., Edelbrock, C., & Smallish, L.
(1991). The adolescent outcome of hyperactive children
diagnosed by research criteria--III. Mother-child
interactions, family conflicts, and maternal
psychopathology. Journal of Child Psychology and
Psychiatry, 32, 233-255.

Baum, C., & Forehand, R. (1981). Long term follow-up
assessment of parent training by use of multiple
outcome measures. Behavior Therapy, 12, 643-652.

Behar, L., & Stringfield, S. (1974). A behavior rating scale
for the preschool child. Developmental Psychology, 10,
601-610.

172

Bierman, K. L, Miller, C. L., & Stabb, S. D. (1987). Improving the social behavior and peer acceptance of rejected boys: Effects of social skill training with instructions and prohibitions. Journal of Consulting and Clinical Psychology, 55, 194-200.

Boggs, S. R., Eyberg, S. M., & Reynolds, L. A. (1990). Concurrent validity of the Eyberg Child Behavior Inventory. Journal of Clinical Child Psychology, 19, 75-78.

Breiner, J., & Forehand, R. (1981). An assessment of the effects of parent training on clinic-referred children's school behavior. Behavioral Assessment, 3, 31-42.

Campbell, S. B., (1985). Hyperactivity in preschoolers: Correlates and prognostic implications. Clinical Psychology Review, 5, 405-428.

Campbell, S. B., & Ewing, L. J. (1990). Follow-up of hard-to-manage preschoolers: Adjustment at age 9 and predictors of continuing symptoms. Journal of Child Psychiatry, 31, 871-889.

Campbell, S. B., March, C. L., Pierce, E. W., Ewing, L. J., & Szumowski, E. K., (1991). Hard-to-manage preschool boys: Family context and the stability of externalizing behavior. Journal of Abnormal Child Psychology, 19, 301-318.

Cantwell, D. P., & Baker, L. (1991). Association between Attention Deficit-Hyperactivity Disorder and learning disorders. Journal of Learning Disabilities, 24, 88-95.

Compas, B. E., Howell, D. C., Phares, V., Williams, R. A., & Giunta, C. T. (1989). Risk factors for emotional/behavioral problems in young adolescents: A prospective analysis of adolescent and parental stress and symptoms. Journal of Consulting and Clinical Psychology, 57, 732-740.

Conners, C. K. (1969). A teacher rating scale for use in drug studies with children. American Journal of Psychiatry, 126, 884-888.

Conners, C. K. (1970). Symptom patterns and hyperkinetic, neurotic, and normal children. Child Development, 41, 667-682.

Cox, W. D., & Matthews, C. O. (1977). Parent group education: What does it do for the children. Journal of School Psychology, 15, 358-361.

Crowther, J. H., Bond, L. A., & Rolf, J. E. (1981). The incidence, prevalence, and severity of behavior disorders among preschool-aged children in day care. Journal of Abnormal Child Psychology, 9, 23-42.

Dadds, M. R., & McHugh, T. A. (1992). Social support and treatment outcome in behavioral family therapy for child conduct problems. Journal of Consulting and Clinical Psychology, 60, 252-259.

Dumas, J. E. & Wahler, R. G. (1983). Predictors of treatment outcome in parent training: Mother insularity and socioeconomic disadvantage. Behavioral Assessment, 5, 310-313.

Edelbrock, C., & Reed, M. L. (1984). Reliability and concurrent validity of the Teacher Version of the Child Behavior Profile. Unpublished manuscript, University of Pittsburgh.

Eisenstadt, T. H., Eyberg, S., McNeil, C. B., Newcomb, K., & Funderburk, B. (in press). Parent-child interaction therapy with behavior problem children: Relative effectiveness of two stages and overall treatment outcome. Journal of Clinical Child Psychology.

Eyberg, S. M. (1988). Parent-Child Interaction Therapy: Integration of traditional and behavioral concerns. Child & Family Behavior Therapy, 10, 33-46.

Eyberg, S. M. (1992). Parent and teacher behavior inventories for the assessment of conduct problem behaviors in children. In L. Vandecreek, S. Knapp, & T. L. Jackson (Eds.), Innovations in clinical practice: A source book (Vol. 11. Sarasota, FL: Professional Resource Exchange.

Eyberg, S. M., & Boggs, S. R. (1989a). Parent training for oppositional preschoolers. In C. E. Schaefer & J. M. Briesmeister (Eds.), Handbook of parent training: Parents as cotherapists for children's behavior problems (pp. 105-132). New York: Wiley.

Eyberg, S. M., & Boggs, S. R. (1989b, November). Psychometric update on the Eyberg Child Behavior Inventory. Paper presented at the annual meeting of the AABT Preconference on Social Learning and the Family. Washington, DC.

Eyberg, S. M., & Johnson, S. M. (1974). Multiple assessment of behavior modification with families: Effects of contingency contracting and order of treated problems. Journal of Consulting and Clinical Psychology, 42, 594-606.

Eyberg, S. M., & Matarazzo, R. G. (1980). Training parents as therapists: A comparison between individual parent-child interaction training and parent group didactic training. Journal of Clinical Psychology, 36, 492-499.

Eyberg, S. M., & Robinson, E. A. (1982). Parent-child interaction training: Effects on family functioning. Journal of Clinical Child Psychology, 11, 130-137.

Eyberg, S. M., & Robinson, E. A. (1983). Conduct problem behavior: Standardization of a behavioral rating scale with adolescents. Journal of Clinical Child Psychology, 12, 347-354.

Eyberg, S. M., & Ross, A. W. (1978). Assessment of child behavior problems: The validation of a new inventory. Journal of Clinical Child Psychology, 7, 113-116.

Fischer, M., Barkley, R. A., Edelbrock, C. S., & Smallish, L. (1990). The adolescent outcome of hyperactive children diagnosed by research criteria: II. Academic, attentional, and neuropsychological status. Journal of Consulting and Clinical Psychology, 58, 580-588.

Forehand, R., & Atkeson, B. M. (1977). Generality of treatment effects with parents as therapists: A review of assessment and implementation procedures. Behavior Therapy, 8, 575-593.

Forehand, R., Sturgis, E., McMahon, R., Aguar, D., Green, K., Wells, K., & Breiner, J. (1979). Parent behavioral training to modify child noncompliance: Treatment generalization across time and from home to school. Behavior Modification, 3, 3-25.

Forehand, R., Wells, K. C., & Griest, D. L. (1980). An examination of the social validity of a parent training program. Behavior Therapy, 11, 488-502.

Funderburk, B. W., & Eyberg, S. M. (1989). Psychometric characteristics of the Sutter-Eyberg Student Behavior Inventory: A school behavior rating scale for use with preschool children. Behavioral Assessment, 11, 297-313.

Funderburk, B. W., Eyberg, S. M., & Behar, L. (1993). Behavior problems in preschoolers: Psychometric evaluation of parent and teacher rating scales. Manuscript submitted for publication.

Goyette, C. H., Conners, C. K., & Ulrich, R. F. (1978). Normative data on Revised Conners Parent and Teacher Rating Scales. Journal of Abnormal Child Psychology, 6, 221-136.

Hechtman, L., (1989). Attention-Deficit Hyperactivity Disorder in adolescence and adulthood: An updated follow-up. Psychiatric Annals, 19, 597-603.

Hollingshead, A. B. (1975). Four factor index of social status. Unpublished manuscript, Dept. of Sociology, Yale University, P.O. Box 1965, New Haven, CT. 06520.

Holm, S. (1979). A simple sequentially rejective multiple test procedure. Scandinavian Journal of Statistics, 6, 65-70.

Hops, H. (1987). Behavior correlates of positive and negative sociometric status among same-sex children. (Available from the Oregon Research Institute, 149 W. 12th Avenue, Eugene, OR 97401).

Horn, W. F., Ialongo, N., Greenberg, G., Packard, T., & Smith-Winberry, C. (1990). Additive effects of behavioral parent training and self-control therapy with attention deficit hyperactivity disordered children. Journal of Clinical Child Psychology, 19, 98-110.

Hughes, R. C. & Wilson, P. H. (1988). Behavioral parent training: Contingency management versus communication skills training with or without the participation of the child. Child & Family Behavior Therapy, 10, 11-23.

Humphreys, L., Forehand, R., McMahon, R., & Roberts, M. (1978). Parent behavioral training to modify child noncompliance: Effects on untreated siblings. Journal of Behavior Therapy and Experimental Psychiatry, 9, 235-238.

Ialongo, N. S., Horn, W. F., Pascoe, M. P. H., Greenberg, G., Packard, T., Lopez, M., Wagner, A., & Puttler, L. (1993). The effects of a multimodal intervention with Attention-deficit Hyperactivity Disorder children: A 9-month followup. Journal of the American Academy of Child and Adolescent Psychiatry, 32, 182-189.

Johnson, S. M., Bolstad, O. D., & Lobitz, G. K. (1976). Generalization and contrast phenomena in behavior modification with children. In E. J. Mash, L. A. Hamerlynck, & L. C. Handy (Eds.), Behavior modification and families. New York: Brunner/Mazel.

Johnson, S. M., & Christensen, A. (1975). Multiple criteria follow-up of behavior modification with families. Journal of Abnormal Child Psychology, 3, 135-153.

Kazdin, A. (1987). Treatment of antisocial behavior in children: Current status and future directions. Psychological Bulletin, 102, 187-203.

Kazdin, A. E., Bass, D., Ayers, W. A., & Rodgers, A. (1990). Empirical and clinical focus of child and adolescent psychotherapy research. Journal of Consulting and Clinical Psychology, 58, 729-740.

Kendall, P. C., & Grove, W. M. (1988). Normative comparisons in therapy outcome. Behavioral Assessment, 10, 147-158.

Kendall, P. C., & Koehler, C. (1985). Outcome evaluation in child behavior therapy: Methodological and conceptual issues. In P. H. Bornstein & A. E. Kazdin (Eds.), Handbook of behavior therapy with children (pp. 75 - 121). Homewood, IL: Dorsey Press.

Kendall, P. C., Lerner, R. M., & Craighead, W. E. (1984). Human development and intervention in childhood psychopathology. Child Development, 55, 71-82.

Kendall, P. C. & Wilcox, L. E. (1979). Self-control in children: Development of a rating scale. Journal of Consulting and Clinical Psychology, 47, 1020-1029.

Knapp, P. A. & Deluty, R. H. (1989). Relative effectiveness of two behavioral parent training programs. Journal of Clinical Child Psychology, 18, 314-322.

Loeber, R. (1982). The stability of antisocial and delinquent child beahvior: A review. Child Development, 53, 1431-1446.

Mannuzza, S., Gittelman Klein, R., & Addalli, K. A. (1991). Young adult mental status of hyperactive boys and their brothers: A prospective follow-up study. Journal of the American Adademy of Child and Adolescent Psychiatry, 30, 743-751.

Mannuzza, S., Klein, R. G., Bonagura, N., Malloy, P., Giampino, T. L., & Addalli, K. A. (1991). Hyperactive boys almost grown up. Archives of General Psychiatry, 48, 77-83.

Mash, E. J., & Terdal, L. G. (1977). After the dance is over: Some issues and suggestions for follow-up assessment in behavior psychology. Psychological Reports, 41, 1287-1308.

McMahon, R. J., & Wells, K. C. (1989). Conduct disorders. In E. J. Mash & R. A. Barkley (Eds.), Treatment of childhood disorders. New York: Guilford.

McNeil, C. B., Eyberg, S., Eisenstadt, T. H., Newcomb, K., & Funderburk, B. (1991). Parent-child interaction therapy with behavior problem children: Generalization of treatment effects to the school setting. Journal of Clinical Child Psychology, 20, 140-151.

Newcomb, K., Eyberg, S. M., Bodiford, C. A., Eisenstadt, T. H., & Funderburk, B. W. (1989, August). SESBI and classroom behavior observations. Paper presented at the annual meeting of the American Psychological Association, New Orleans.

Packard, T., Robinson, E. A., & Grove, D. C. (1983). The effect of training procedures on the maintenance of parental relationship building skills. Journal of Clinical Child Psychology, 12, 181-186.

Patterson, G. R. (1982). Coercive family process. Eugene, OR: Castalia.

Peed, S., Roberts, M., & Forehand, R. (1977). Evaluation of the effectiveness of a standardized parent training program in altering the interaction of mothers and their noncompliant children. Behavior Modification, 1, 323-350.

Pfiffner, l. J., Jouriles, E. N., Brown, M. M., Etscheidt, M. A., & Kelly, J. A. (1990). Effects of problem-solving therapy on outcomes of parent training for single-parent families. Child & Family Behavior Therapy, 12, 1-11.

Pisterman, S., Firestone, P., McGrath, P., Goodman, J. T., Webster, I., Mallory, R., & Goffin, B. (1992). The role of parent training in treatment of preschoolers with ADDH. American Journal of Orthopsychiatry, 62, 397-408.

Pisterman, S., McGrath, P., Firestone, P., Goodman, J. T., Webster, I., & Mallory, R. (1989). Outcome of parent-mediated treatment of preschoolers with Attention Deficit Disorder with Hyperactivity. Journal of Consulting and Clinical Psychology, 57, 628-635.

Prinz, R. J., O'Connor, P. A., & Wilson, C. C. (1981). Hyperactive and aggressive behaviors in childhood: Intertwined dimensions. Journal of Abnormal Child Psychology, 9, 287-295.

Richman, N., Stevenson, J., & Graham, P. J. (1982). Preschool to school: A behavioral study. London: Academic.

Robins, L. N. (1978). Sturdy childhood predictors of adult antisocial behaviour: Replications from longitudinal studies. Psychological Medicine, 8, 611-622.

Robins, L. N. (1981). Epidemiological approaches to natural history research: Antisocial disorders in children. Journal of the American Academy of Child Psychiatry, 20, 556-580.

Robinson, E. A., & Eyberg, S. M. (1981). The Dyadic Parent-Child Interaction Coding System: Standardization and validation. Journal of Consulting and Clinical Psychology, 49, 245-250.

Robinson, E. A., Eyberg, S. M., & Ross, A. W. (1980) The standardization of an inventory of child conduct problem behaviors. Journal of Clinical Child Psychology, 9, 22-29.

Sayger, T. V., & Horne, A. M. (1987, August). The maintenance of treatment effects for families with aggressive boys participating in social learning family therapy. Paper presented at the annual meeting of the American Psychological Association, New York, NY.

Schaughency, E. A., Hurley, L. K., Yano, K. E., Seeley, J., & Talarico, B. (1989, August). Psychometric properties of the SESBI with clinic-referred children. Paper presented at the annual meeting of the American Psychological Association, New Orleans.

Sloane, H. N., Endo, G. T., Hawkes, T. W., & Jenson, W. R. (1991). Improving child compliance through self-instructional parent training materials. Child & Family Behavior Therapy, 12, 39-64.

Sosna, T. D., Ladish, C., Warner, D., & Burns, G. L. (1989, August). Psychometric properties of the SESBI in a preschool sample. Paper presented at the annual meeting of the American Psychological Association, New Orleans.

Spivack, G., & Swift, M. (1967). Devereux Elementary School Behavior Rating Scale manual. Devon, PA: The Devereux Foundation Press.

Strain, P. S., Steele, P., Ellis, T., & Timm, M. A. (1982). Long-term effects of oppositional child treatment with mothers as therapists and therapist trainers. Journal of Applied Behavior Analysis, 15, 163-169.

Strayhorn, J. M. & Weidman, C. S. (1989). Reduction of attention deficit and internalizing symptoms in preschoolers through parent-child interaction training. Journal of the American Academy of Child and Adolescent Psychiatry, 28, 888-896.

Strayhorn, J. M. & Weidman, C. S. (1991). Follow-up one year after parent-child interaction training: Effects on behavior of preschool children. American Academy of Child and Adolescent Psychiatry, 30, 138-143.

Sutter, J., & Eyberg, S. M. (1984). Sutter-Eyberg Student Behavior Inventory. (Available from Sheila Eyberg, Dept. of Clinical & Health Psychology, Box J-165, JHMHC, University of Florida, Gainesville, FL 32610)

Taylor, W. F., & Hoedt, K. C. (1974). Classroom-related behavior problems: Counsel parents, teachers, or children? Journal of Counseling Psychology, 21, 3-8.

Tremblay, R. E., McCord, J., Boileau, H., Charlebois, C. G., Le Blanc, M., & Larivee, S. (1991). Can disruptive boys be helped to become competent? Psychiatry, 54, 148-161.

Verhulst, F. C. & Van Der Ende, J. (1991). Four-year follow-up of teacher-reported problem behaviours. Psychological Medicine, 21, 965-977.

Wahler, R. G. (1980). The insular mother: Her problems in parent-child treatment. Journal of Applied Behavior Analysis, 13, 207-219.

Walker, H. M. (1970). The Walker Problem Behavior Identification Checklist. Test and manual. Los Angeles: Western Psychological Service, Inc.

Walker, H. M., & Hops, H. (1976). Use of normative peer data as a standard for evaluating classroom treatment effects. Journal of Applied Behavior Analysis, 9, 159-168.

Walker, H. M., & McConnell, S. (1987). The Walker-McConnell scale of social competence and school adjustment. Austin, Texas: Pro-Ed.

Walker, H. M., Shinn, M. R., O'Neill, R. E., & Ramsey, E. (1987). A longitudinal assessment of the development of antisocial behavior in boys: Rationale, methodology, and first year results. Remedial and Special Education, 8, 7-16.

Webster-Stratton, C. (1982). Teaching mothers through videotaped modeling to change their children's behavior. Journal of Pediatric Psychology, 7, 279-294.

Webster-Stratton, C. (1984). Randomized trial of two parent-training programs for families with conduct disordered children. Journal of Consulting and Clinical Psychology, 52, 666-678.

Webster-Stratton (1992). Individually administered videotape parent training: "Who benefits?" Cognitive Therapy and Research, 16, 31-35.

Webster-Stratton, C., & Eyberg, S. (1982). Child temperament: Relationship with child behavior problems and parent-child interactions. Journal of Clinical Child Psychology, 11, 123-129.

Webster-Stratton, C. & Hammond, M. (1990). Predictors of treatment outcome in parent training for families with conduct problem children. Behavior Therapy, 21, 319-337.

Webster-Stratton, C., Hollinsworth, T., & Kolpacoff, M. (1989). The long-term effectiveness and clinical significance of three cost-effective training programs for families with conduct problem children. Journal of Consulting and Clinical Psychology, 57, 550-553.

Webster-Stratton, C., Kolpacoff, M., & Hollinsworth, T. (1988). Self-administered videotape therapy for families with conduct-problem children: Comparison with two cost-effective treatments and a control group. Journal of Consulting and Clinical Psychology, 56, 558-566.

Weiss, G., & Hechtman, L. T. (1986). Hyperactive children grown up. New York: Guilford.

Weisz, J. R., Weiss, B., Alicke, M. D., & Klotz, M. L. (1987). Effectiveness of psychotherapy with children and adolescents: A meta-analysis for clinicians. Journal of Consulting and Clinical Psychology, 55, 542-549.

Wells, K. C., & Egan, J. (1988). Social learning and systems family therapy for childhood oppositional disorder: Comparative treatment outcome. Comprehensive Psychiatry, 29, 138-146.

Wells, K. C., & Forehand, R. (1985). Conduct and oppositional disorders. In P. H. Bornstein & A. E. Kazdin (Eds.), Handbook of clinical behavior therapy with children (pp. 218-265). Homewood, IL: Dorsey Press.

Whalen, C. K., & Henker, B. (1991). Therapies for hyperactive children: comparisons, combinations, and compromises. Journal of Consulting and Clinical Psychology, 59, 126-137.

Wolfe, D. A., Sandler, J., & Kaufman, K. (1981). A competency-based parent training program for child abusers. Journal of Consulting and Clinical Psychology, 49, 633-640.

Beverly White Funderburk was born on March 27, 1959, in Norlina, North Carolina, to James and Ann White. She graduated from Warren Academy in June 1977. Beverly attended the University of North Carolina at Chapel Hill, from which she received a Bachelor of Arts degree with honors in psychology in 1981. After college, Beverly spent four years in Chapel Hill, North Carolina, working in the field of children's mental health. Positions held included group home manager in a facility for children with mental retardation, home-bound educational aide, and program director of Annie Sullivan Enterprises, a nonprofit agency serving children with behavioral disturbances. In August 1985 Beverly entered the clinical psychology program at the University of Florida. She was granted an M.S. in clinical psychology in April 1988 after completing a master's thesis entitled "Standardization of a Behavior Rating Scale with Preschool Children." Beverly completed a clinical internship in 1990 and 1991 at the University of Florida Department of Clinical and Health Psychology, with a specialization in medical psychology. Beverly's major professional interests are in pediatric psychology, with an emphasis on treatment of behavioral disorders in young children. Beverly has a husband, Chuck Funderburk, who is an orthopaedic surgeon specializing in sports medicine and hand surgery, and they have one son, Chase.

I certify that I have read this study and that in my
opinion it conforms to acceptable standards of scholarly
presentation and is fully adequate, in scope and quality, as
a dissertation for the degree of Doctor of Philosophy.

Sheila M. Eyberg, Chair
Professor of Clinical and
Health Psychology

I certify that I have read this study and that in my
opinion it conforms to acceptable standards of scholarly
presentation and is fully adequate, in scope and quality, as
a dissertation for the degree of Doctor of Philosophy.

Russell M. Bauer
Associate Professor of
Clinical and Health Psychology

I certify that I have read this study and that in my
opinion it conforms to acceptable standards of scholarly
presentation and is fully adequate, in scope and quality, as
a dissertation for the degree of Doctor of Philosophy.

Stephen R. Boggs
Assistant Professor of
Clinical and Health Psychology

I certify that I have read this study and that in my
opinion it conforms to acceptable standards of scholarly
presentation and is fully adequate, in scope and quality, as
a dissertation for the degree of Doctor of Philosophy.

Suzanne B. Johnson
Professor of Clinical and
Health Psychology

I certify that I have read this study and that in my opinion it conforms to acceptable standards of scholarly presentation and is fully adequate, in scope and quality, as a dissertation for the degree of Doctor of Philosophy.

Jane F. Pendergast
Associate Scientist of
Statistics

This dissertation was subjected to the Graduate Faculty of the College of Health Related Professions and to the Graduate School and was accepted as partial fulfillment of the requirements for the degree of Doctor of Philosophy.

August, 1993

Dean, College of Health
Related Professions

Dean, Graduate School

CPSIA information can be obtained
at www.ICGtesting.com
Printed in the USA
LVHW040836110219
607106LV00004B/260/P